AQUINAS ACADEMY
1945-2015

Text copyright © 2016 remains with the author

All rights reserved. Except for any fair dealing permitted under the Copyright Act, no part of this book may be reproduced by any means without prior permission. Inquiries should be made to the publisher.

National Library of Australia Cataloguing-in-Publication entry
Creator: Thorpe, Julie Anne, author.
Title: Aquinas Academy 1945-2015 : a very personal Australian story / Julie Anne Thorpe.

ISBN: 9781925486148 (paperback)
9781925486155 (hardback)
9781925486162 (ebook : epub)
9781925486179 (ebook : Kindle)
9781925486186 (ebook : pdf)

Series: Marist series ; no. 7.
Notes: Includes index.

Subjects: Aquinas Academy (Sydney, N.S.W.)--History.
Marist Fathers. Province of Australia.
Catholic Church--Adult education--New South Wales--Sydney--History.
Adult education--New South Wales--Sydney--History.

Dewey Number: 378.07129441

The Marist Series
Through the Marist Series the Society of Mary (Marist Fathers) shares projects by Marists in the field of theology and history and works about the role of the Marists in the church, in particular in the Pacific.
Series Editor: Alois Greiler SM
1. *Catholic Beginnings in Oceania: Marist Missionary Perspectives*, 2009, edited by Alois Greiler SM.
2. *A Mission Too Far. . . Pacific Commitment and the Missions 1835–1841*, 2012, Jan Snijders SM.
3. *Thinking Things Through: Essays in Philosophy and Christian Faith*, 2102, Andrew Murray SM.
4. *Verguet's Sketchbook*, 2014, Mervyn Duffy SM and Alois Greiler SM.
5. *Letters from the Marist Missionaries in Oceania 1836-1854, 2016*, Charles Girard SM.
6. *Thinking about Political Things: an Aristotelian Approach to Pacific Life*, 2016, Andrew Murray SM.

Cover design and Layout by Astrid Sengkey
Original artwork by Liz McQueen used with permission

Text Minion Pro Size 10 &11

Published by:

An imprint of the ATF Ltd.
PO Box 504
Hindmarsh, SA 5007
ABN 90 116 359 963
www.atfpress.com
Making a lasting difference

AQUINAS ACADEMY
1945-2015

A Very Personal Australian Story

Julie Thorpe

ATF Theology
Adelaide
2016

Table of Contents

Foreword	vii
1. Founding Stones	1
2. A Mother's Son	9
3. Wartime Academy	17
4. The People's Bread	29
5. Academicians	41
6. A Priest and a Politician	51
7. Seeing in the Dark	63
8. Going to Rome	71
9. After Thomas	87
10. Christian Growth	95
11. New Faces	109
12. Mary's Song	119
13. Handing on the Faith	129
14. A Mystical Heart	139
15. Nazareth	149
Timeline of an Academy	155
Acknowledgements	157
Index	161

Foreword

Those who have worked in adult education for any length of time are aware that the stories of the people who come to learn are the heart of the educational process. This is particularly the case at Aquinas Academy where the focus is not so much information as it is formation. It is entirely correct to say that Aquinas Academy is people and their individual stories—their stories of searching and questioning, stories of longing and wondering, stories of discovery and decision-making.

Aquinas Academy has been a gathering place since March 1945. The gatherings and the stories that constitute the Aquinas Academy do not stand alone however. The history of anything bears some relationship to the history of everything. Aquinas Academy is a microcosm of both church and world. I will mention just two of the stories that bear this out.

Firstly, the story of Fr Austin Woodbury SM—affectionately known as 'The Doc'—is obviously front and centre. When I arrived at the Marist Fathers' seminary, Toongabbie, in 1965 as a teenager, Aquinas Academy had been running for twenty years. 'The Doc' was a legend, though the telling of that legend varied amongst Marists. I am personally gratefully to Dr Julie Thorpe for the way she has told 'The Doc's' story. She has done that with great care—care for the facts, care for the person. She has done justice to the memory of a good Marist.

Secondly, there is a story that is hinted at rather than fully told. It is the story of the proposal for a Catholic university in Sydney. 'The Doc' was, at one stage in the early 1950s, engaged in serious discussions concerning the possibility of the Aquinas Academy becoming the faculty of philosophy in a Catholic university. Was this proposal for a Catholic university vision or over-reach? There were certainly some in the wider community thought it was the latter. But 'The Doc', the Archbishop of Sydney and the Apostolic delegate and at least one Marist provincial all seemed rather sanguine about the project at the time. In any event, it never got off the ground.

The history of the Aquinas Academy is worth telling for more reasons than the stories themselves. Yves Congar wrote: 'Acquiring knowledge of history is the sure way of acquiring confidence in the church. History teaches that nothing is new, and that the church has survived sadder and more difficult situations. History is a school of wisdom and of limitless patience.' (Cited by Thomas O'Meara *America*, 5 Feb 1994, v170, n4428, 16.)

We are blessed to have had Dr Julie Thorpe write this history of Aquinas Academy. She is not only a professional historian with a very impressive academic background, she has a poet's sensitivity to those things that are so easily misrepresented by factual prose. People come alive in her text. To read this work of history is to encounter a representative group of those people—a very large number, too many to name and contact personally—who will forever be known as the Aquinas Academy.

Michael Whelan SM, PhD
Director
December 2015

1
Founding Stones

Signs for fresh spinach and pumpkin skirt the mountain pass. Mandarins and manure lie roadside for sale like the old homesteads built by generations who settled on the Hawkesbury. Maloneys, Shakeshafts, Doyles, Donovans, Woodburys: their names written in stone at the mountain's foot in the cemetery of Spencer's tiny Catholic church. William Woodbury donated the land for the church to be built after he and his fourteen children became Catholic. Now four rows of his descendants lie with him and his wife, Mary, overlooking Mangrove Creek.

I am looking for William and Mary's teenage granddaughter, Theresa. I find her parents, side by side, nearby her older brothers, two young nephews, a niece and twin great-nieces who left, like her, before their time. I find her at last in front of her grandparents. I feel the metallic roughness on the smooth stone under my hand as I trace the copper letters of her life: her three names, Theresa Catherine Woodbury, a precise death on 6 September 1914, an exact age of fourteen and a half. Letters in stone normally spell an ending, inked in a book and grieved for a lifetime, but her death over a century ago marks the beginning of this story.

When I first discovered Theresa's memorial card in the archive of the Marist priest and founder of the Aquinas Academy, Austin M Woodbury, I knew only her name and the dates of her birth and her death. There was no photograph of her on the memorial card, just a black and white image of a scourged Christ crowned with thorns and the Latin inscription, *Ecce homo*: 'Behold the man.' I had seen the same image on a holy card signed on the back, 'To Austin, Theresa,' with no date. I wondered at this girl's closeness to a priest who kept her handwriting on a holy card with the memorial card inside his breviary. They must have been the same Theresa, a sister or cousin with the same surname? But the obituaries I read at first didn't mention a sister called Theresa. Then I found sleeved inside a folder of family memorabilia a photograph of a girl about thirteen or fourteen in a white dress with dark hair and eyes. Finally a three-paged document of Austin's early life written by his brother, Leo, mentioned an unnamed 'beautiful young sister' they lost in 1914.

Gradually with the help of Austin's nieces and nephew I pieced together the threads of Theresa's life and death. She was at boarding school when her appendix burst. Word travelled slowly by river post and slower still after war broke out in Europe in August. The news of a sick girl with acute peritonitis didn't reach her parents until after their daughter was dead. There were no obituaries for children in 1914, but a weekly chronicle in the *Windsor and Richmond Gazette* I found in a digital newspaper archive expressed deep regret along the river at the sudden death of Theresa Woodbury in the Convent of Mercy, Goulburn. The remains, the notice said, were transported by water to the chapel at Spencer where 'the funeral was a large and representative one.'

Austin was at home helping his father and older brothers on the orchard, loading citrus to be ferried down the river to Brooklyn then train to Sydney, when the news of her death arrived. He was fifteen and a half, closest in age to Theresa, twelve months and one day apart. In the birth order of eleven children who all survived past infancy, he was seventh and she was eighth. A few months after her death he began studying Latin by correspondence from Sydney. He may already have been considering the priesthood before her death. The holy card might have been a clue to his vocation she'd encouraged. He'd begun reading English Catholic authors Hilaire Belloc and GK Chesterton as well as the encyclicals of Pope Leo XIII before leaving school at fourteen to work on the family farm. He could have lodged his Latin application the winter before she died, but it seemed her absence inspired his calling. The hidden threads of her life and death were woven inside a priest's vestments.

Silent threads of lost lives shaped the cloth of my formation in the Catholic tradition. Trained in empirical methods of history I turned to other ways of naming the unspeakable past. Historian Jay Winter calls these creative acts of mourning 'liturgical silences' as distinct from other kinds of political, essentialist or familial silences. Silences that are liturgical, he says, seek to remember something or someone as sacred. To mourn means, etymologically, to care for the past. So liturgical silences are sacraments of care, creative acts that bear witness to an irrecoverable past. They are visible signs of what is beyond reach yet close enough to touch.

The invitation to write a history of the Aquinas Academy came in the guise of another liturgical silence. Michael Whelan, a Marist priest and principal of the Aquinas Academy for the past sixteen years, approached me after an evening lecture in a course on spirituality he taught with Marie Biddle, a Sister of St Joseph. Two weeks earlier I had told him in the coffee break about my decision to leave an academic career. He told me he had grappled with his priesthood in his mid thirties, but knew in his gut he did belong even if he didn't fit the institutional church that had ordained him. The topic of that evening's lecture had been the idealised roles and identities that replace or mask our true selves: the careers, relationships or religious vocations that can come irreparably undone in a crisis or death of something precious. Life does not recover.

Michael's offer two weeks later was like the gift of stone. I was *leaving* stories of the past behind, stepping into an unknown future and starting to think I'd been deluded by poets and super-moon apparitions. That's *why* I'd turned up for a course on spirituality, why I'd confessed my decision to a Catholic priest during a coffee break. I tried to circle away from the stone. I had no experience in Australian religious history, firstly. My doctorate was in Austrian history and I'd only taught modern European. Secondly, I was barely Catholic. I avoided the term convert, which sounded like a foreign currency machine, but I had been received into the Catholic church a year after I completed my doctorate and it was a tradition I was beginning to feel at home in even if I didn't fit either. Thirdly, though I didn't say this to Michael, I had never worked for a priest. He told me to think about it: the job might just turn into a gift.

I did say yes, the next day, and thank you. It wasn't ingratitude as much as shock at the sheer gratuitousness of something I couldn't grasp as a gift. I wasn't ready to trust and, like ancient Zechariah at the news of his impending parenthood, I was struck silent. I had to learn to bear witness all over again.

'Before you learn the tender gravity of kindness,' poet Naomi Shihab Nye says, 'before you know kindness as the deepest thing inside / you must know sorrow as the other deepest thing. / You must wake up with sorrow. / You must speak to it till your voice / catches the thread of all sorrows / and you see the size of the cloth.'

I decided to start listening to the threads. Until I could see the size of the cloth.

Three years after Theresa's death, the Woodbury family faced another tragedy: the death of Austin's twenty-three-year-old brother, Stephen, in Flanders in 1917. According to the records of the Australian war memorial, Stephen embarked from Sydney for overseas service in November 1916. His eldest brother, Herbert, kept one of the last letters Stephen wrote. It was dated 20 February 1917 and addressed from Camp Durrington, Wiltshire.

I have heard and read the family stories of the Woodbury brothers playing cricket for Spencer as far west as Glenorie. They all reckoned Steve could have been an Australian fast-bowler. But the letter he wrote to Herbert five months before his death reveals a keen diplomatic mind with an interest in banking and parliament. He mentioned the rumour of America entering the war, the failed peace note, newspapers full of the 1917 war loan and everywhere the talk of victory. 'It is marvellous how confident they are that it will end this summer.' He asked after Herbert's plans to branch out on his own and signed off 'hoping for better times.'

The family was told that Stephen's body was found with a prayer of Saint Ignatius of Loyola in his tunic pocket. He'd picked up a copy of the prayer a few days before he was killed at Gapaard on 31 July, the feast day of Saint Ignatius. The date became hallowed for the Woodbury family when Austin was ordained to the priesthood in Rome on exactly the same day his brother had been killed ten years earlier.

Because Stephen is one of the sixty-two thousand Australians who died in the First World War, his name will be projected onto the night time wall of the capital's monument to the dead thirty times for thirty seconds over four years of a nation's mourning. For fifteen minutes

Stephen Woodbury will light the parade of remembrance all the way to parliament. School children will recite his name and age inside the cloister.

Stephen's name, I found out when I visited the war memorial, is only a few panels from my great-great-great uncle, William Hitchen, who died aged fifty-two in the same war. I could reach Stephen with my fingers above my head between Wilson and Woodgate. William was waist high between Hinton and Hobbs. Someone standing next to me was on his phone checking the spelling of his lost relative. John Ignatius Mooney from Goulburn was remembered in the Last Post ceremony for the day. Named after Saint Ignatius, he died in France a year after Stephen was killed in Belgium on Saint Ignatius's feast day. Maybe John Mooney had a younger sister who was taught by the same Sisters of Mercy in Goulburn who kept vigil at the bedside of Stephen's younger sister, Theresa, before she died.

Austin was eighteen when Stephen was killed. He didn't think any more Australians would be called up for service so, six months after Stephen's death, Austin left home to enter the Marist junior seminary, Montbel, in Hunters Hill and begin his nine years of preparation for the priesthood. Around the time Stephen enlisted for the war Austin had made contact with a couple of Marist priests who had visited his family church in Spencer. He spoke to one of them, James Monaghan, about his desire to become a priest. Perhaps he mentioned Theresa's death, his Latin studies, his love of Chesterton, his work on the family orchard, Stephen's departure for Europe. Monaghan had taught at the Montbel juniorate since it opened in 1911. He introduced Austin to the rector, John Rausch, a Luxembourger who spoke English, French, German and Latin and had been a missionary in the Solomon Islands before arriving in Sydney. Lessons, prayers and gardening were the rule of the day for the handful of pupils Austin joined.

The following year the juniorate transferred to Mittagong, a redbrick house on forty acres with fir trees and fruit orchards opposite the Mittagong farm homes for children and down the road from the Marist brothers' juniorate and novitiate. Austin breathed highland air for the first time since his family's double loss. He thrived in his studies. His intermediate grades were published in the *Sydney Morning Herald* with other country school results: A in History, Latin, French, Maths I and II and a B in English. The orange trees were a taste of his Hawkesbury home. There were leisurely afternoon walks twice weekly, maybe a weekend cricket match on the oval of the Marist brothers' juniorate where Catholic boys from the farm homes attended mass in the chapel they'd built with their own bricks.

At the end of 1919, just after Austin's intermediate exams, Monaghan was transferred to Queensland leaving Rausch to take all the subjects as well as being chaplain to the Marist brothers. Austin was co-opted to teach maths, history and English while Rausch taught Latin and French. There is no documentary evidence he was teaching his peers at the age of twenty, only his mention of it decades later in an interview with fellow Marist Tony King. Whatever the nature of his early teaching experience, one-to-one tutoring or classroom lecturing, a bond between the European teacher and his protégé lasted for some years after Woodbury left Mittagong at the end of 1920 to enter the Marist novitiate in Greenmeadows in New Zealand with another pupil, David Murray.

Woodbury was professed at twenty-three in the Society of Mary at Mount St Mary's seminary in Greenmeadows. He wrote afterwards in a letter to the New Zealand Marist provincial, John Holley: 'To live a life worthy of so special a son of Mary is a thing quite beyond our powers, save in so far as these are assisted and uplifted by the help which comes from on high and which is obtained by prayer.' He told Holley he was looking forward especially to his studies in philosophy 'for there is no study which I have ever followed, which I like so well as philosophy.'

The year of Woodbury's profession coincided with an encyclical by Pope Pius XI on the study of philosophy according to Thomas Aquinas, the thirteenth-century Dominican friar and saint. *Studiorum Ducem* ('Higher Studies') was published in 1923 to mark the sixth centenary of the canonisation of Saint Thomas. It followed Pope Leo XIII's 1879 encyclical, *Aeterni Patris* ('On the Restoration of Christian Philosophy'), which mandated the teaching of Thomistic theology and philosophy in Catholic seminaries throughout the world. Woodbury would have read it along with the rest of Leo XIII's encyclicals as a teenager.

In his 1923 encyclical Pius XI addressed Woodbury and every seminarian: if 'a man devotes himself to the investigation of the supernatural, he will find a powerful incentive in such a pursuit to lead a perfect life; for the learning of such sublime things, the beauty of which is a ravishing ecstasy, so far from being a solitary or sterile occupation, must be said to be on the contrary most practical.' The pope referred to Saint Thomas with both his honorific titles of 'angelic' and 'common' doctor of the church and reminded seminarians that the end of studying theology and philosophy was not knowledge for its own gain, but 'to bring us into close living intimacy with God.' Amid the aftermath of the First World War and the rise of the Italian Fascist state, Pius XI mentioned the writings of Aquinas on 'the lawful power of the state or the nation, natural and international law, peace and war, justice and property, laws and the obedience they command, the duty of helping individual citizens in their need and co-operating with all to secure the prosperity of the state, both in the natural and the supernatural order.' He wished especially for a wider study of Aquinas's teaching on international law 'for it contains the foundations of a genuine "League of Nations."' Saint Thomas was also a writer of sacred songs, the pope added. Woodbury's beloved Chesterton later quipped in his biography of Saint Thomas that he 'devoted his whole life to documenting whole systems of Pagan and Christian literature; and occasionally wrote a hymn like a man taking a holiday.' Pius XI concluded his encyclical with the prayer of Saint Thomas: 'You who make eloquent the tongues of little children, fashion my words and pour upon my lips the grace of Your benediction. Grant me penetration to understand, capacity to retain, method and facility in study, subtlety in interpretation and abundant grace of expression.'

Three years after his profession Woodbury followed the pope's words all the way to Rome to study at Saint Thomas's own university, the Angelicum. He wrote to Rausch in March 1926: 'I am chosen to make a trip to the city of the Caesars to study theology there. This is a very great chance of getting a higher education in theology and it is partly owing to the help you gave me in my studies at Montbel and Mittagong that I have been able to see this chance within my reach.'

He came home to Spencer to farewell his family before his departure for Rome twelve years after Theresa was buried near her grandparents' graves.

In death Theresa and Austin lie only three rows apart, but in living memory whole systems of family and church separate them. Mourned by her mother and father in their lifetime, half forgotten by nieces and nephews with their own families to mind, there isn't anyone left to tend the memory of a departed daughter and sister with no descendants of her own. I feel the unfairness of a girl robbed of a life choice. Her married brothers and their wives have children to care for their graves. Her four sisters who entered religious life are buried with their communities. One married sister is buried with a husband and a daughter. Stephen has a nation to mourn him. Austin left behind alumni to remember his name. Two vases of purple silk flowers stand beside his headstone that reads: 'Beloved Founder & Teacher, Aquinas Academy, Sydney.' There are silk flowers on their parents' graves and two red silk poppies in front of the plaque for Stephen.

Four bull ants crawl across the cold tiles of Theresa's grave. I have come with nothing to lay here, not even a single stone. If I was in a church I'd light a candle, but there is only a pile of discarded silk flowers in a corner of the cemetery. I pick through green plastic stems and then, on the other side of the barbed wire fence, I spot a purple wildflower on its own. Carefully I pluck it between the wire, carry its fresh sap in my fingers, pour water from my bottle onto the grass at the foot of Theresa Woodbury's grave and leave my wildflower in the moistened earth.

2
A Mother's Son

Austin Woodbury's black and white photograph hangs on the wall of the Aquinas Academy he founded, high forehead with sharp eyes fixed slightly above and to the left of the camera's gaze. This is the famous philosophy teacher his students dubbed 'the Doc' for his two degrees from the pope.

I am drawn to a different photograph: a sepia Sidney Riley studio print of Woodbury on the eve of his departure for Rome. In his mid twenties, he looks more like a young soldier smiling so that loved ones will be able to hold the memory of his face over the long months of separation with no known return. It is the face of a beloved son and brother, carrying his family's joys and sorrows, the youngest son of a mother who had already buried in her heart a daughter to illness and a son to war.

'My darling son,' Margaret Woodbury wrote to Austin a few days after he sailed from Sydney in September 1926 on the *Orama*. She tracked the month-long voyage in the shipping news while he jotted down the sights in a diary. He arrived in Rome on 21 October and spent his 'first night in the eternal city.' A week later he was at St Peter's for the consecration of six Chinese bishops by Pope Pius XI. 'Very close to the Holy Father,' he wrote in his diary. 'Much impressed by the appearance of the Holy Father; a much more refined and delicate face than his portraits had led me to believe, with much more of humanity and understanding and human kindness in it; a face also of high intelligence.' He sent his mother a clipping from the *Catholic Universe* about the consecration and wrote in red above the article: 'When I first saw the Pope.'

Since he had left home almost nine years earlier, letters between them had travelled up and down the Hawkesbury first to Hunters Hill then Mittagong, across the Tasman to Greenmeadows and, now, over the oceans to Rome. But this separation was sensed more deeply. Margaret was going blind. Her letters after Austin's last departure are written in the crooked hand of a mother left in the darkness of diabetes and her children's deaths.

Anxious about his mother's rapid decline and with his ordination approaching at the end of July, Woodbury wrote to his former teacher, Rausch, to see if Daniel Hurley, the new parish priest at St Patrick's, Church Hill, would invite his father for dinner to celebrate his first mass. His parents had moved to Sydney to live with their married daughter and Woodbury thought a presbytery meal might provide welcome distraction and much needed respite from the constant care for Margaret at home. He offered his first mass for his mother and sent her souvenirs of his ordination. He posted a papal relic of Pius X, a holy card blessed by Pius XI, wrote postcards showing his university cloister 'where we stroll and argue for a few minutes between lectures.' Weaving the sacred thread of relics and cards and prayers between them to keep her alive.

'Your letters are always welcome and cheer me up very much and give me something to think about,' she wrote in January 1928. Despite her deteriorating health and eyesight she continued to relay news of family, floods and federal elections, worried about his workload and sicknesses and passed on recipes for a tonic to cure his repeated bouts of bronchitis. In February she wrote to wish him a happy birthday and asked about his plans to travel to England and France after his exams. She wanted to send him 'a few pounds' for his trip. She wrote again in April telling him to 'take care of your throat my boy and the time won't go fast enough for me until your return.' She asked for prayer—for herself and her son—from the mother of God, and signed off across the continents with 'oceans of love.' In her last letters to him at the end of June she sent prayers for his exams and twenty-three pounds for his trip: 'It was the best I could do.'

Margaret wasn't able to travel to Stephen's war grave like some Australian mothers and fathers after the war, so perhaps her precious pounds to Austin were her very own pilgrimage to the place of her son's death. Hughena Hunter went twice to France to remember her two sons, Reginald and Hector, killed in the war. The Australian war memorial has the soil she brought home from France where Reginald was buried. When the Menin Gate memorial was unveiled in Ypres for soldiers with no known grave like Stephen, a week before Austin was ordained in Rome on the tenth anniversary of Stephen's death, Margaret received a double consolation: Austin's priesthood and Stephen's name at rest on a wall of memory. The following year after his exams Austin travelled to Belgium in search of Stephen's name. His older brother, Leo, recalled years later that Austin had walked for miles through the military cemetery looking for a cross with Stephen's name. He finally found him on the honour roll with other Australians on the Menin Gate. He had studied the pope's face in person, but now at the end of his trip he came face to face with his brother's name written in stone.

Austin arrived home in time for Christmas to find his mother bedridden and her sight completely gone. The weeks following his return were her greatest joy and his deepest pain. He was granted permission by the archbishop to celebrate mass and give her communion in the home every day until she died on 9 February 1929. The lost son had returned to feed the one who had fed him. He had come home to her but she was blind to him. It was his first experience of administering the rites of death and burial.

The death of Margaret at fifty-eight was a devastating loss for the family, already shattered by the deaths of Theresa and Stephen. But Austin suffered a deeper wound knowing that his mother never saw him fulfill his religious vocation. Her obituaries are glued into the front pages of the scrapbooks that hold newspaper clippings and articles he published. It was a wound he carried for the rest of his life. Years later he wrote to a family friend, 'I returned from Rome and she was not able to see me as a priest.'

Burying his grief in work, Woodbury returned to New Zealand to teach at the Marist secondary college, St Patrick's, in Wellington. He threw himself into public lectures and preaching on top of his teaching load. Less than a month after his mother's death, he gave a lecture to the Catholic University Students' Guild in Wellington on the doctrine of Action Française, the right-wing political movement spearheaded by Charles Maurras whose journal Pius XI had placed on the church's index of prohibited books. Woodbury's eloquent disentangling of Maurras from Thomism for an antipodean audience stamped the young lecturer fresh from doctoral studies in Rome with the approval he needed in the raw absence of a mother.

His two years in Europe had given Woodbury heady exposure to some painful political splits between Catholic intellectuals. The French Jesuit and cardinal, Louis Billot, who taught theology at the Gregorian University where Woodbury attended his lectures, resigned as cardinal in 1927 in support of Action Française. Woodbury would have read Billot during his seminary studies in New Zealand. A fortnight after his arrival in Rome, Woodbury recorded his awe at meeting the great theologian in a diary entry in November 1926. 'Long I have desired to see him,' he wrote of Billot saying benediction at evening devotions for the feast of Saint Stanislaus Kostka at the church of St Andrea del Quirinale. 'He walks with his head bent right down over his chest, the back of his head being almost at right angles with his spine; but he walks rapidly; had a few words with him after the ceremony, as he sat in the Sacristy.'

After the papal censure of Maurras's movement, Woodbury expressed his admiration for Billot's intellectual brilliance in a letter to Rausch. 'In some respects I would have preferred to have gone to the Gregorian,' Woodbury wrote in February 1928, 'yet I see now that the Angelic[um] has some advantages; it at least gives a better grasp and acquaintance with the theology of Saint Thomas, with its inexhaustible richness. Yet on many questions I have not abandoned Billot, and still regard him as by far the best mind in recent theology.'

Woodbury's own doctoral supervisor at the Angelicum, the French Dominican Réginald Garrigou-Lagrange, fell out with his friend and fellow Thomist, Jacques Maritain, over political events in France and Spain. Garrigou-Lagrange had been appointed in 1917 to Rome's first chair for spirituality and held public lectures on mystical theology at the Angelicum every Saturday of the academic year until he retired in 1959. He was a sought out spiritual director in addition to his courses on Aristotelian metaphysics and fundamental theology. Maritain and Garrigou-Lagrange had both been students of philosophy at the Sorbonne, but were reacquainted after Maritain and his wife, Raïssa, became Catholic. In Paris Jacques and Raïssa founded the Thomist study circles devoted to the thought of Thomas Aquinas and approached Garrigou-Lagrange to be director of their annual Thomist retreats. The Maritains and Garrigou-Lagrange established an intellectual and spiritual companionship that eventually became strained by Jacques's increasingly public opposition to Maurras and Franco. More hurtfully for Raïssa, who was Russian Jewish by birth and had published a history of Judaism, Garrigou-Lagrange's attacks on Jews and philo-Semitic Catholic intellectuals finally estranged the couple from their former mentor.

Woodbury had been an admirer of Maritain since his undergraduate days at Greenmeadows. His exercise books from St Mary's contain published reviews of Maritain's 1920 *Art and Scholasticism*, on which Jacques and Raïssa collaborated although Jacques didn't acknowledge his wife's full contribution until after her death. One reviewer hailed the book as 'something sane, rational, profound, and yet clear with a luminous beauty.' Another observed that 'within the structure of medieval philosophy art and beauty have their place, being really so much a part of that structure that they cannot be segregated. It is M. Maritain's purpose to explain what this philosophy was.' It was also a purpose Woodbury made his own.

In his Wellington lecture, Woodbury took up the theme of art and beauty in defining the doctrinal conflict between the Catholic church and Action Française. Maurras and his followers were devoted to 'the cult of the beautiful,' Woodbury said, whose custodians they held to be Christianity and the European tradition. But they confused Christianity with the church, which taught the transcendent beauty of sanctification as the ultimate end of human life and not the finite end of aesthetic perfection. It was the church that 'begot the burning poetry of Dante, and the Gothic architecture, and the stained glass of Chartres, and the immaterial loveliness attained by Fra Angelico, and Ghiberti's doors in Florence, and the terra-cotta of Luca Della Robbia,' Woodbury tripped through treasures he'd visited like a black and white slideshow of western art. 'While therefore the Catholic does not differ from the adherent of the Action Française in his view of what the Church has meant and means to Europe,' Woodbury continued, 'he differs from him by a vast abyss in his doctrine of what the end of the Church is. As the Church is not European, because not human, in her origin so she is not European, because not earthly, in her end.' The papal condemnation of Action Française was a painful necessity prompted by 'not so much the state of mind of a person who receives an injury from a recognised enemy, as the feeling that one has on receiving a vital wound from one whom one has flattered oneself that one has befriended.' The church, he concluded, 'has a transcendent necessity to be faithful to her divine commission, and must not shrink even at sometimes hurting those who serve her out of love, not to speak of those who would magnify her in order to use her for purposes that are theirs but not hers.'

He was at the peak of his intellectual and personal power, combining his love of Thomistic thought on beauty with his vision for teaching the laity that seeded during the next decade in his work to establish a Catholic academy for lay education. His audience in Wellington was Catholic university students, not seminarians, and in this respect of educating lay Catholics he stood closer to Maritain, the Catholic philosopher of civil society, than Garrigou-Lagrange, the Roman gatekeeper of Thomism before the Second Vatican Council. Woodbury's style and content was all Garrigou-Lagrange, but in fostering lay minds, including unmarried women and women religious at a time when women religious received only rudimentary theological education, his vision was more akin to the Maritains' Thomist study circles than the cloister.

Woodbury kept a foot in the European door that had opened up his intellectual horizons, but in 1931 he was felled by further tragedy. After returning to teach at the seminary at Greenmeadows where he had been a novice, Woodbury narrowly escaped death in the Napier earthquake that crushed a group of priests and students inside the chapel. He had been with them but left to take a phone call. He came back to find the chapel gutted and had to crawl over bodies to get them out of the rubble and anoint the dying and the dead. Nine were killed and many more injured. Woodbury was barely thirty, ministering to his students two years after his mother's death.

Four decades after the earthquake he recounted harrowing scenes in an interview with Tony King. The transcript reads like a tape replaying the wreckage of buildings and bodies over and over with one vivid memory of a seventeen-year-old nun killed in a convent down the road from the seminary seeming to evoke the death of his sister, Theresa. 'There were three nuns in the little Convent at Greenmeadows,' Woodbury recalled, 'and there was one little postulant, it was her first day teaching.' Some of the surviving students from the seminary went down to the convent and found the nuns 'lying down under the rubble, holding hands, three of them abreast and the one in between, the centre one, was the little postulant and she was dead, the other two were alive. That was her first day teaching,' he repeated, 'she was only seventeen and it was at the morning tea break at the Convent, at the school, morning tea break, eleven o'clock break or something, whatever it was and the nuns were in having a cup of tea and they ran out and the building got them as they were going out and the three of them were abreast, all holding hands, the little girl in the middle.' It was a Tuesday morning, he remembered, and it had all happened 'about thirteen minutes to eleven.'

His world shattered again, Woodbury wrote home to his brother, Leo, that he 'could lay down and die' for the loss of his students. Woodbury was suffering severe physical and emotional shock but continued teaching while doing weekend relief work in rural parishes until he had a complete collapse in his health with a heart attack at the age of thirty-seven. He came back to Sydney to recuperate and began making plans to open the first Marist seminary in Australia on a bare ten acreage at Toongabbie. Transforming fertile wasteland into feeding ground for young minds Woodbury found, after so much personal trauma, at last his life's work.

3
Wartime Academy

When Woodbury arrived home, wholly depleted, he turned to what was most familiar to restore his strength and spirit for the long haul ahead: farming and his family. In Sydney he was reunited with his younger sister, Cecily, back from overseas missionary service. She had entered the Daughters of Our Lady of the Sacred Heart in Kensington when he was in Mittagong and was working in the Pacific islands when Margaret died. After the Toongabbie seminary opened in 1938, Cecily took over her mother's role of correspondent, writing to Austin about his health and feeding him news about her life in the missions during the Pacific war.

'My dearest Brother,' she wrote from Butaritari, 'I wrote to you last in Nov[ember] but I am wondering if it ever reached its destination or if it went to the bottom of the sea.' If post by sea was a perilous venture in wartime, invocations were most efficacious. She reported the miraculous survival of one of her missionary sisters aboard a bombed ship en route to Nauru and sent prayers from the local school children for the new seminary in Toongabbie. Cecily wrote to Austin on the eleventh anniversary of their mother's death after rereading 'your long letter of that sad February.' She was delighted to hear from Austin that a coral tree had been planted at the seminary in memory of Margaret: 'Where she is she brings peace and joy.'

Woodbury set his seminarians to work planting red gums, eucalypts and citrus in the dairy flats of Toongabbie. When he wasn't teaching, Woodbury spent holidays and weekends up at Spencer with his oldest brothers, Herbert and Aloysius, discussing cows. Toongabbie became a working dairy farm as Woodbury learnt to multitask: metaphysics and calving, often during the same lecture. It was strenuous labour and although Woodbury was frequently unwell, gaining a reputation for hypochondria in the infirmary, Toongabbie equipped him with experience in fundraising and public relations that he would need beyond the classroom in his quest to create Australia's first Catholic university.

The idea for a Catholic school of philosophy and theology for the laity stemmed from Woodbury's post-doctoral year in Wellington and took root in his imagination while on staff at Greenmeadows. He approached Hurley with the idea when Hurley became the New Zealand Marist provincial. Hurley told him to keep it on the backburner for the time being. He had plans for a separate Australian Marist province and was appointed provincial of the new Australian province at the end of 1938. After Woodbury stepped down as rector of Toongabbie at the end of 1943 he again put his proposal to Hurley, who agreed to support it and seek endorsement from the archbishop.

Woodbury was sixteen years younger than the New Zealand-born Hurley and was unfazed by his older confrère, who intimidated other Marists. Hurley was small fry beside the likes of Billot and Garrigou-Lagrange. Woodbury was in Rome by the time Hurley was appointed parish priest at St Patrick's, but he still managed to solicit an invitation from Hurley for his father to celebrate his ordination. Although it was Rausch who was closest to Woodbury and his family, Hurley would have been on hand after Woodbury's return at the time of his mother's death in Sydney. When Hurley was made the New Zealand provincial and later Australian provincial he became Woodbury's direct superior, setting a pattern for the next several years of Woodbury's forays into adult education and, on a few occasions, politics.

Woodbury had toed the papal line on Action Française when others, including his supervisor Garrigou-Lagrange, were tightlipped about the validity of the censure. But he was less politically astute on the question of fascism more generally in Europe. In July 1937, after returning to New Zealand to teach for a year at the boarding school of St Patrick's secondary college in Silverstream and still recovering from his heart attack the previous year, Woodbury was forced to defend his outburst at another Marist priest, Higgins, in a meeting at which Hurley was present as provincial. While Woodbury didn't detail Higgins's accusation against him in a letter he wrote to Hurley the week after the meeting took place, the threefold distinction Woodbury drew between the Fascist Party, an ideology, and a social, political and economic programme suggests the accusation referred to Woodbury's ideas about right wing movements that had been his topic at the Catholic Students' Guild in Wellington eight years earlier.

Forming minds in the Thomist tradition and running a dairy farm appears not to have sidetracked Woodbury's interest in European politics during his six-year term as rector at Toongabbie. In September 1940 he wrote a pamphlet called 'The Corporative State' adapting for Australia the ideas of the late Austrian chancellor, Engelbert Dollfuss, and forwarded it to Archbishop Gilroy for ecclesiastical approval. The ten-page pamphlet explained the differences between fascism and 'the genuine corporative system' based on Catholic political, social and economic thought and included a diagram showing the lines of the 'corporational hierarchy' from the president down to the chancellor, the cabinet, the various councils of state, culture and economy, the professional corporations or syndicates of fishery, finance, transport, agriculture and medicine, the occupational corporations or guilds of wheat, dairy, poultry, sheep and fruit, the regional guilds of New South Wales, Queensland, Victoria, Tasmania, Western Australia and South Australia, the various districts which Woodbury named for New South Wales as North Coast, Middle Coast, South Coast, Western and Riverina, to the local guilds within each district at the base of the hierarchy, such as the Newcastle, Parramatta, Penrith and Windsor guilds of the Middle Coast. Woodbury concluded his pamphlet with 'the beautiful words of Dollfuss' in a translated extract from the Austrian Catholic newspaper, *Die Reichspost*, of a speech the chancellor made less than three months before his assassination in July 1934 by Austrian Nazis. Gilroy sent the pamphlet back stamped in black ink with a *nihil obstat* signed by Eris O'Brien, archdiocesan director of the lay apostolate, Catholic Action, who noted in the marginalia that Pope Pius XI had condemned the Italian corporative model in his 1931 encyclical, *Non abbiamo bisogno* ('We do not need'), and encouraged vocational groups rather than corporative ideas as the basis for Catholic Action. Gilroy assured Woodbury the typescript was 'interesting and instructive, but does not need an Imprimatur.'

I couldn't tell where Woodbury got hold of the German-language newspaper or its translation, or what source he used to study the Austrian state under Dollfuss and his successor, Kurt Schuschnigg, when I came across the pamphlet amongst Woodbury's correspondence. What was clear from my own doctoral study of the dictatorship Dollfuss established in 1933 was Woodbury's political naïveté in claiming its 'Catholic' basis was applicable to the Australian context and his seeking ecclesiastical support for this claim. But he wasn't the only one swept up in the politics of Dollfuss's death: the Catholic press around the world hailed the diminutive Austrian chancellor as a martyr in the struggle against National Socialism. In Sydney, the *Catholic Freeman's Journal* gave coverage to his death and the requiem mass in St Mary's cathedral at which Daniel Hurley, then parish priest at St Patrick's, served as deacon. Dollfuss's 'beautiful words' in 1934 gave no indication of his government's incarceration of social democrats in a prison camp leaving their families destitute, nor the anti-Semitic legislation the state enacted against Austrian Jews in the professional and civil services, nor the opposition of the Austrian Catholic bishops to the state's indoctrination of young Catholic minds and souls in the Austrian youth organisation modelled on Italian Fascist brigades. When Austria was annexed in 1938 to Nazi Germany, Hitler took over an already fascist and anti-Semitic state.

Woodbury was still joining in the political fray after he stepped down from the Toongabbie seminary to prepare for the work of educating lay Catholics. At the beginning of 1944 he entered his second novitiate in Hunters Hill where he had begun his Marist formation twenty-six years earlier. It was to be a time of spiritual renewal and reflection on all that lay behind and ahead. In September that year he delivered a social justice sermon at St Patrick's that received wide coverage in the Catholic press. The *Catholic Weekly* printed an abridgement of the sermon that argued, among other points, for the federal government to finance coalminers' co-operatives against union efforts to nationalise mines. Class warfare in the mines would then be abolished, Woodbury said. 'The miner would have an incentive to work. Hope would be introduced into his life. He would feel a new dignity and a new interest. He would be in large measure his own master. He would feel himself on the way to economic independence and to that political freedom which is citizenship.' Politically Woodbury was out of his depth, but in his style of courting ecclesiastical authority and readers of the Catholic press Woodbury was honing his skills for running an academy in the city instead of a seminary on a dairy farm.

In January 1945 Woodbury chose the annual communion breakfast of the Catholic Journalists' Guild, in the presence of Archbishop Gilroy, to launch his vision for an academy of philosophy and theology in Sydney. The late Pope Pius XI had declared Francis de Sales the patron saint of writers and journalists in 1923, the same year as his encyclical on Saint Thomas Aquinas. In Woodbury's seven-page speech to Sydney's Catholic journalists he made the case for Saint Thomas, reminding his audience that the vocation of the journalist was 'to restore the mind of your fellow men in Christ.' He elaborated on what Jacques Maritain diagnosed as the modern 'sickness of the mind.' This sickness was not the rejection of reason, Woodbury said, but 'the weakening of intellect,' which according to Saint Thomas, 'is higher than reason.' The loss of the ability to distinguish, to assess and to discern, Woodbury summed up, was the loss of what Aristotle called 'a spark of the divine.' The result? 'You gnaw like a rat at the pillars of society.' So to remedy the epidemic of rats in Sydney and to rediscover the divine spark of the modern mind, the Aquinas Academy would become an 'institute at which young men and women of the professions, of the public services, of the various institutions of post-school education, teachers and others, might be made acquainted with the profound wisdom of the great Catholic masters of philosophy, and thereby be fitted for the role of guides unto the minds of Australians.'

The *Catholic Weekly* announced the inauguration of the Aquinas Academy in Sydney in its editorial for 25 January 1945, 'Catholic Education Advances.' 'The magnificent system of Catholic school education has given Catholic children a fundamental grounding in Catholic knowledge and culture, but the lack of post-school education,' the editorial said, 'has meant that there has been lacking Catholic laymen with a complete Catholic education, equipped fully for the task of bringing a powerful Catholic impress to bear on secular society.' Growing interest among the laity in discussion groups and books was heartening, the newspaper noted, but such an unsystematic approach boded 'signs of dilettantism and skin-deep study in the mighty subjects of the Catholic religion.' The newspaper echoed Woodbury's call for an Academy for all educations. 'University graduates, teachers, professional men, industrial leaders, journalists, all can be assisted by the education offered by the new Academy,' and hoped that the laity would not only support the Academy, but would have further incentive to do so through accreditation of the study courses on offer.

While Sydney's Catholic journalists applauded the vision and raised the academic stakes to the level of university accreditation, the archbishop offered the man at the helm his 'very cordial approval' and, Gilroy added, in a line that Woodbury must have relished over and over in the years to come, an episcopal blessing. 'By establishing an Academy in which a sound knowledge of Scholastic Philosophy may be obtained by studious members of the Clergy, Religious and Laity, you will be conferring a great benefit upon the Church and the State.'

The only formality left was the final administrative tick from the leadership of the Australian province of the Society of Mary. Hurley had already pledged his support pending the archbishop's. On 7 February 1945 at the Toongabbie seminary, Hurley signed off on behalf of the provincial education committee. His secretary and co-signatory, David Murray, had known Woodbury since their juniorate days and taught with him at St Patrick's in Wellington the year after Woodbury returned from Rome. Woodbury was present at the meeting and probably drafted the document. 'It was resolved, gratefully acknowledging the approval of the Cardinal-Archbishop of Sydney for the establishment of a school of Philosophy and allied subjects in Sydney available to the general public,'—the statement elevated Gilroy to the cardinalate before the official announcement from Rome at the end of that year—'that such a school be instituted forthwith, to teach philosophy and kindred disciplines, according to the principles, doctrine and method of Saint Thomas Aquinas, such school to be named "Aquinas Academy," and a Marist Father to be its immediate controller with the title of "Regent."' Now it was over to the forty-five-year-old Regent Woodbury to deliver on his dream almost sixteen years to the day since his mother had died.

Sister Patricia Woodbury greeted me through the intercom as I pushed open the gate. I walked through a rosemary garden to the top of the path where she welcomed me in wide arms, although we had only spoken once on the phone. I could feel her strong bones. We entered the small living room and I sat at the dining table while she put on the kettle.

I recognised her table instantly. It could have been my grandmother's. I knew exactly how to behave at this table. Sometimes I think grandmothers should run the church. There would be no pulpits, and no processions except for crawling infants and unaccompanied children who make their way to the front to sit in their grandmother's lap. Then we would all eat buttered jatz biscuits with slices of cheese and green pickled onions, and milk would be poured out from the lip of a jug.

Sister Patricia carried the coffee to the table. A Dominican nun for almost seventy years, she chatted for a few moments about the research I had begun. Then she started her story.

It was Christmas 1944. She was sixteen, fresh out of boarding school in Sydney. Her uncle Austin was on the verandah of her Spencer home persuading her father, Aloysius, to let Patricia go down to Sydney to work as his secretary. The archbishop had offered Woodbury the Gloucester Street war storerooms of the Catholic United Services Auxiliary as premises for the new academy. Students had already begun to enroll for the first term's classes that were scheduled to begin on 7 March, the feast day of Saint Thomas Aquinas. Woodbury still needed a typist. He had no money to pay her, but he knew a family she could board with in Ramsgate. And the parish at St Patrick's had a girls' basketball team Patricia could play in, so she'd have friendly young people to meet.

'I was not asked, but told I s'pose,' she smiled, eyes creasing.

At sixteen, she was beginning her own adult education. It was a rude start. There wasn't any money to buy chairs for the office so she had to sit on fruit crates to type up her uncle's notes.

'We just had a little room,' she said, 'with a table in it. He sat on one side with his typewriter and I sat on the other side with my typewriter. We had all boxes and things around for his books,' she waved her arms around the table where we were sitting. 'And just outside there was a little servery and that's where we served the supper from.' Sometimes she stayed on for the first class and served cups of coffee during the break to the students. But her uncle made sure she left before dark, so she rarely stayed for the second class after supper.

Because there was a wartime shortage of paper and ink, Patricia had to duplicate the lecture notes next door at St Patrick's business college, which the Sisters of Mercy ran. 'I went in there one Friday afternoon and copied off all the notes and for some reason I came in on the Saturday.' Perhaps she'd planned to meet up with some of the parish youth, or play in the girls' basketball team. 'Sister Philomena was waiting at the door for me so I came up to her and she said I'd left the machine turned on.'

'You got in trouble?' I asked.

'I never did it again.'

I was at her table to find out what became of that teenage typist who forgot to turn off a Gestetner during a war. I also wanted to know more about her uncle beyond the archives of ink and stone. Sitting at her table eating and drinking with her I felt immediately drawn inside an archive of flesh and blood as if her story was the entrance hall to an expanded ancestral imagination filled with shelves of other stories I could only glimpse from their spine. Patricia's story coming of age at the end of a war, like her aunt Theresa's death at the beginning of another war, opened up space between the lines of institutional memories written down by journalists, prelates and priests.

Peace came to the Pacific on 15 August 1945, the day after Patricia turned seventeen. 'I was so happy and excited when Uncle Austin suggested we go down to Martin Place.' I wished I could see a photograph of her at seventeen walking through the crowds of Sydney with her tall uncle. 'The place was electric with excitement and thanksgiving—the war was over. You could hear parents saying, *My son will be coming back to us soon.* You could almost hear the anxiety lift from their shoulders. The noise was deafening and flags were flying everywhere.'

The *Catholic Weekly* gave front-page coverage to the peace declaration on the Feast of the Assumption. Eighty thousand Catholics visited St Mary's cathedral, the newspaper said, bells rang for the eleven o'clock mass and Sydney's Catholics streamed in all day to light candles and say the rosary. Photographs showed service men and women in uniform kneeling at the Altar of Our Lady and 'business girls,' like Patricia Woodbury, 'unexpectedly freed from work, pinned handkerchiefs on their heads as they entered the cathedral.'

The electricity in Martin Place triggered memories of Patricia's uncle Stephen killed twenty-eight years earlier. 'I was very conscious of Uncle Austin reliving that time,' she told me. 'We stayed down there for a while and then he put me on the train to go home and made sure I was on the train.'

I wondered what other painful memories stirred unspoken between them. Patricia was the same age as the young postulant killed in the Napier earthquake. She had been just a few months old when her grandmother, Margaret, died. She told me that her uncle used to visit her at her Dominican boarding school while he was rector at Toongabbie. Perhaps she reminded him of his own sister, Theresa, who died at boarding school. I wondered, too, not for the first time, about the hidden thread between grief and vocation.

'I was sitting opposite him one day and I said to him that I was going to enter the Dominicans,' she paused. 'There was dead silence. Then he got up and walked around behind my chair, and walked around and walked around, and he said, *I am so happy*.'

I asked about the influences on her decision.

'I had seven aunts as nuns.' Aside from her aunt Cecily in the Pacific, she had three other nuns on her father's side. Her mother had three sisters in the Little Company of Mary. The Dominican nuns who taught her in Sydney had a convent at Maitland and that was where she eventually entered before becoming a primary school teacher. Her uncle Austin preached the sermon at her reception of the habit a year before her first profession as a Dominican in December 1948.

Three years later she lost a young brother, Matthew John, drowned accidentally on Boxing Day. He was fourteen, the same age as Theresa when she died.

I already knew that he drowned and the date. The week before we met I had thumbed through a family tree trying to arrange in my head birth orders, deaths, marriages, religious professions, children and their children's children, some my own age. Later I found his grave in the Spencer cemetery, four rows in front of Theresa's, next to his parents.

'I'd just been finally professed,' she said folding her corner of the tablecloth over and back on itself. Final profession, three years after making her temporary vows, was her perpetual pledge to God in the religious life.

She was twenty-three. Her uncle Austin was the person who rang the convent to tell her superior.

'They didn't tell me that night and next morning while we were saying Office, the superior kept on getting up and going out and I thought, *Oh she must be terribly sick*, and then at the end of mass she got up again and went straight out and I thought, *Gosh the poor thing*. And then I went off, we all went off to breakfast after mass and I hurried up because some of the nuns were going on holidays that day and I was helping them bring down their luggage. And the next thing I get a message to come to her office, and she sits me down and reads it to me out of the paper.'

'Out of the paper?'

'That's what she was getting up and going out and getting the paper so nobody else'd see it.'

'It was on the front page?'

'No, it was inside the paper. But she didn't want anybody else to open it up and see it.'

Listening to the tape later I tried to picture her reading, but couldn't.

'And all I could say when she read it out, I said, *Is he dead?* I just didn't comprehend it. And then I got upset because we could have had mass for him.'

She wasn't allowed to go to the funeral, since convent rules forbade home visits, but she could go down to Sydney to her old boarding school for her parents to come and see her. Eventually.

'We nearly lost Mum at that stage, too.'

She wasn't looking at me anymore.

'She had a heart attack.'

'Just after it happened?'

'Yeah, but we were so fortunate that the body was found.'

I was still trying to put her sentences together. She meant her brother.

'You didn't get to celebrate Christmas with your family so you weren't there when it happened. You were always with your community.'

I stopped.

'And your mother recovered?'

'Oh yes, she lived till—she died in 1975.'

Another silence.

'But anyhow it took its toll on them,' she continued. 'We had to get Uncle Austin to come up to Dad.'

Her father had sown new fruit trees that year for his youngest son to take over.

'He was called Matthew John, but everybody called him John except Dad. He called him Matt. And he was going around saying, *Poor Matt, poor Matt.* Uncle Austin came up and talked to him and he settled down a bit after that. Uncle Austin said the mass of course.'

'It sounds like your uncle had a way of being a presence in the family,' I started again.

'He had a big influence on us, I think,' she responded. 'And going through all that I think it made him really compassionate.'

'I'm sure it's also affected your ability to relate to people in your work,' I reflected back to her. I knew that after teaching she had retrained in pastoral care, accompanying grieving families and helping them prepare for funerals.

'I think so. I think I learnt a lot from Uncle Austin,' she said. 'How to cope with these kind of things.'

'Did he talk about the things he'd experienced?' I asked.

'No, he didn't talk about them but I could see from the way he interacted with other people that his compassion came through all the time,' she replied. 'I think I was able to take that on board.'

Her words had slowed over the conversation.

'It's a strange thing,' she spoke softly, 'every morning at mass, I pray for a compassionate heart. And I think that's all come from him.'

In three years, Sister Patricia Woodbury will celebrate her seventieth jubilee as a Dominican. Seventy years is a long time, I think, to learn to love.

4
The People's Bread

News of the fledgling Aquinas Academy travelled by word of mouth and Woodbury's own publicity channels from country towns to London and Rome during the postwar years. The bishops of New South Wales congratulated Woodbury on his achievements after he wrote to them at the end of 1945 to promote enrollments for the following year. 'Even if the numbers do not increase, and they probably will, you will be turning out twenty really educated men every year,' wrote the bishop of Wagga Wagga. The attendance of 'over a hundred at the lectures in this first year,' the bishop of Bathurst said, 'is a fine beginning, and is an augury of even greater things.' He intended to promote the Academy to students of St Stanislaus college leaving for university. The bishop of Wilcannia-Forbes also shared his concern about the influence of a secular university education on Catholic students and saw the Academy's work as 'a substitute for that which so many of us have long desired to see eventuate, a Chair of Scholastic Philosophy at the University of Sydney.'

The subject of the bishops' concerns was the Scottish professor of philosophy at the University of Sydney and founding president of the Freethought Society, John Anderson. In April 1943 Anderson provoked political outcry in the New South Wales parliament after his public lecture to the New Education Fellowship claiming that clergy and religion didn't belong in education. Politicians in both the lower and upper houses carried a vote of censure against Anderson. The upper house forwarded it to the university senate, which sent a reply back to parliament that the motion stifled 'the spirit of free inquiry' at the university. The *Catholic Weekly* published a reply to Anderson by the Jesuit head of St Ignatius' college, Riverview, Noel Hehir, and said in its editorial that free speech was not the issue, but rather Anderson's appointment to 'the nation's highest seat of learning' in an institution founded, according to the preamble to the University and University Colleges Act, 'for the better advancement of religion and morality and the promotion of useful knowledge.' From the pulpit of St Mary's cathedral Reverend Patrick Tuomey's Lenten sermon, reprinted in the *Catholic Weekly*, invoked the wartime sacrifice of 'the mothers of so many of the Billy Ryans, the "Bluey" Truscotts and the Paddy Finucanes,' for whom Anderson's 'atheistic philosophy' offered no consolation in their sons fighting and dying for God and country and who believed that 'even in death there was something more than final darkness and complete extinction.'

Further abroad the appointment in Rome of Daniel Hurley as assistant general of the Society of Mary in 1947 gave Woodbury a European platform for the Academy's work of educating lay minds. Hurley wrote to Woodbury in November 1948 about his visit to the Marist parish in London, St Anne's, where he saw plenty of scope but little clerical vision for teaching the laity. 'Several laymen, business and professional men of London to whom I spoke of the Academy were enthusiastic over it saying that several could be established with success in London. It is sad to see no one ready to break the bread for the children.'

In May 1949 Hurley reported to Woodbury 'a few keen men over here are watching the experiment and wondering if their Provinces will ever undertake anything like it.' Take London again, for example. 'Only lately, I was discussing the matter with a London solicitor who has the keenness and the anxiety of an apostle. He spoke of the depressing state of our Catholic students at the London University and he implored me to use any influence with the Marist Fathers in England and organise something for London. But I am afraid that the idea is too advanced for our men,' Hurley continued his lament about lay children without bread. 'It must be borne in mind that such a work is not a job but an apostolic vocation. Here in Italy it is much the same. Bishops write able pastorals but nothing is done. One man remarked to me recently that it is not paper that the people want but a piece of bread and a roof over their heads. In the meantime, Communism is flourishing because it is the only organisation with a promising programme,' Hurley changed the apostolic mission to the laity to an apocalyptic key. 'When there is no Catholic dynamite the Communists will supply some and end in blowing the social structure to bits.'

Social reconstruction was already on the Academy's agenda. Woodbury's social justice sermon at St Patrick's in September 1944 had drawn prominent coverage in the Catholic press, treading on the turf of Woodbury's contemporary, Dr PJ 'Paddy' Ryan, a Missionary of the Sacred Heart who got his two doctorates from the pope the year after Woodbury left Rome. On his return to Sydney Ryan taught philosophy at the Sacred Heart seminary in Kensington, gave lectures and courses in apologetics and public speaking, wrote pamphlets and spoke on radio. The two philosopher-priests probably crossed paths in Rome during their doctoral studies: Ryan was at the Gregorian University where Woodbury's admired ex-cardinal Billot taught. In 1942 Ryan was appointed director of the Sydney archdiocesan lay apostolate and, in October 1944, started the first Workers' School of Social Reconstruction with Ryan's lecture, 'The Christian Idea of Work,' on page with Woodbury's social justice sermon in the *Catholic Weekly*. After the war, the pair shared personnel and facilities for the Workers' Schools that met at the Academy and Catholic United Services Auxiliary (CUSA) House in Elizabeth Street and were attended by Catholic ex-service men and women.

Woodbury and Ryan were just two of the nearly fifty government and non-government agencies providing education in Sydney alone, the *Catholic Weekly* reported in September 1946. But the Catholic approach was distinct from the secular philosophy of education, the newspaper pointed out, quoting from Pope Pius XI's 1929 encyclical, *Divini Illius Magistri* ('On the Christian Education of Youth'): 'The proper and immediate end of Christian education is to co-operate with divine grace in forming the true and perfect Christian.' Christian education is concerned with the whole of human life, 'physical and spiritual, intellectual and moral, individual, domestic and social' not to diminish life, the encyclical said, 'but in order to elevate, regulate and perfect it in accordance with the example and teaching of Christ.' The 1929 encyclical had been a papal protest against fascist curricula and youth groups that taught war and praised violence, but in 1946 it was turned into a lesson to Catholic readers about the dangers of secularism.

The Workers' Schools expanded and decentralised in 1947 with lectures conducted by the various religious orders around Sydney. 'The monasteries, once centres of learning for the people as well as for intellectuals, might well be so again,' the *Catholic Weekly* observed in April 1947. Courses at the Aquinas Academy 'had particular appeal for specialists, constituting at best a minority of the Catholic community,' but provision for the rest of the Catholic laity was still needed. Branches at Bondi Junction, Eastwood, Marrickville, North Sydney, Randwick as well as the city locations of CUSA House and the Aquinas Academy offered courses for young working men and women that could be expanded in the future to include courses on international and Pacific affairs, modern and Australian history, and English literature.

Students of the Workers' Schools and the Aquinas Academy would have figured in the thirty thousand who showed up at the boxing stadium at Rushcutters Bay in September 1948 to hear Paddy Ryan debate Edgar Ross from the central committee of the Australian Communist Party on the topic, 'That Communism is in the best interests of the Australian people,' with half the audience outside in the rain listening through loudspeakers. They would have been spotted again a few months later in the crowd of sixty thousand Catholics who turned out in scorching January sun, the *Catholic Weekly* said, to hear Cardinal Gilroy in the Domain protest the trial and imprisonment of Hungarian Cardinal Mindszenty.

It was an era when crowds gathered to hear men on wooden boxes. Holding their listeners captive, *spellbound*, we say, as if they became prisoners of a magician the moment they began to listen. I once heard a grandmother, a Holocaust survivor, say it was the most beautiful sight since she'd stepped off the boat to see the Domain, each Sunday on Speaker's Corner, dotted with wooden boxes of freedom, she called it. Beautiful, wooden freedom.

Woodbury weighed in on his own box against Professor Anderson at the start of 1952. 'The department of philosophy in the University of Sydney is a cancer at what ought to be the heart of the scholastic life of this city,' he said at the opening of the Academy year in an address that the *Catholic Weekly* reprinted on its front page. Echoing the bishops of Bathurst and Wilcannia-Forbes, Woodbury warned students and their parents 'that a grave risk to their future intellectual and moral life is incurred by students who follow the course of philosophy at the University of Sydney without at the same time taking the courses at this academy.'

Catholic students were at grave risk in the department of psychology at the University of Sydney as well. The Aquinas Academy had added courses in psychology to its offerings in 1950, but first year university students could still be led astray even by fellow Catholics. Sister Aquinas, principal of Marist Sisters' college in Woolwich, wrote to Woodbury in March 1955 about a former student of the college who had enrolled in psychology at Sydney. Her school teachers had advised her to attend Aquinas Academy courses 'to offset any false notions she might absorb' at university, but she was warned off the Academy by Catholic students in the Newman Society. Sister Aquinas gave Woodbury the student's name and asked him to 'keep an eye on her' in case she did turn up.

Woodbury began gathering evidence against the spiritual advisor to the Newman Society, Roger Pryke, whom Cardinal Gilroy had appointed Catholic chaplain at the University of Sydney. Pryke's chaplaincy appointment in 1951 coincided with the infiltration of BA Santamaria's clandestine anti-communist movement into trade unions and student newspapers with the consent and funds of the Australian episcopate. Paddy Ryan headed the movement in Sydney under Gilroy and encouraged the political tactics of vote rigging at student council meetings. Pryke had a wooden box, too, but his was less public grandstand than cafeteria table where he drank coffee and engaged students with European ideas of the lay apostolate. He was an admirer of Maritain, like Woodbury, and shared Woodbury's passion for the laity, but took issue with the way Thomist philosophy was taught at the Aquinas Academy as if it was the sole doctrine of the Catholic church.

Woodbury submitted his case to Gilroy at the end of 1959 listing allegations against Pryke and another priest, Grove Johnson, who had studied with Pryke in Rome and with whom Pryke had set up a rival school of philosophy, the Lyndhurst Academy. Johnson was purported to have said in front of students, who reported his comments back to Woodbury, 'Dr Woodbury's intellectual development ceased thirty years ago.' Pryke was overheard telling a student that 'there is no danger in the school of philosophy at Sydney University.' The evidence cited against Pryke pointed to a number of Catholic students who had come to Woodbury 'in serious difficulty regarding their faith' and apparently at risk of apostasy. Pryke and Johnson were dismissed from the Lyndhurst Academy and received a cardinal's dressing down. 'I have seen both Father Pryke and Doctor Johnson, and have their assurance that they will not say a word reflecting on the Academy,' Gilroy wrote to Woodbury on Christmas Eve 1959.

The trail of evidence was thin, largely circumstantial, yet sufficiently alarming with at least four cases of apostasy in a single report to the cardinal about the spiritual lives of Catholic students in Sydney. But Woodbury's actions exposed a deeper personal insecurity. Why worry about a charismatic university chaplain when he had the admiration of the pope and the weight of the leading lay Catholic author, Frank Sheed, behind him? Sydney-born Sheed and his English wife and author, Maisie Ward, founding publishers of Sheed and Ward in London, toured Australia in August 1954. During his visit Sheed paid tribute to the Aquinas Academy, calling it 'the most notable achievement in Catholic education in the English-speaking world,' in a statement that the *Catholic Weekly* published to mark the start of the Academy's tenth anniversary year.

Pope Pius XII was also an admirer and Woodbury was on Italian-speaking terms with his diplomatic representative. The apostolic delegate, Paolo Marella, sent Woodbury a papal medal for his silver jubilee as a priest in 1952 with an image of Pius XI, whose face Woodbury had studied up close in Rome and who had blessed a holy card for his blind mother. Marella's successor, Romolo Carboni, gave the address at the start of the Academy year in 1958, telling Woodbury's students to take their ideas, 'warm with zest and love,' and 'scatter them in abundance about the world of your everyday.' He paid the highest tribute to their 'exceptional master and guide,' Woodbury, who 'must rank among the most qualified and penetrating exponents of our time of the teaching and attitudes of the Angelic Master Himself.' Favour came even from Saint Thomas Aquinas upon his eponymous school of philosophy.

When the apostolic delegate and cardinal were unavailable, Woodbury rang in the next down the line. In December 1961 the auxiliary bishop of Sydney, Thomas Muldoon, accepted Woodbury's invitation to preside at the inauguration the following year. It would give him joy, Muldoon ended on a flourish, to open the Aquinas Academy, which is 'eminent as the focal-point of sanity in a mad city.' Muldoon told Woodbury he had submitted a report to the cardinal that included plans for the Academy's expanded role in Catholic higher education in Sydney: '*Quod Deus concedat!* [God grant it!]' signed the auxiliary bishop.

If the children's bread and the perils of communism were uppermost on the minds of the men in London and Rome, and the chair of philosophy at Sydney University the main item of controversy from Macquarie Street to the diocese of Wilcannia-Forbes, what motivated the students themselves who caught trains and buses from their jobs and homes in the suburbs each evening of the week to attend Woodbury's classes in the city? The auxiliary bishop of Sydney might call the Aquinas Academy 'the focal-point of sanity in a mad city,' but how did a twenty-year-old woman, straight out of teachers' college in Armidale, see its central purpose for her life commuting from her state school job in Canley Vale?

It was a picnic of a time, I found out when Elizabeth Sancataldo invited me for lunch. I brought spinach quiche and Elizabeth had bread rolls with butter and cold grapes from the fridge for dessert. On the phone when we had made arrangements she told me she had been part of the Academy social club. When I arrived at her Catholic retirement village her dining table was spread with photo albums and pocket diaries filled up with a black and blue ink social calendar for the five years she attended Woodbury's lectures as a young school teacher from Warren.

'I'd been in Sydney for twelve months,' she began. At home for the Christmas holidays in 1951 a friend of her mother's told her about the Aquinas Academy. 'I'd never even heard of philosophy,' she shrugged. 'When I came back to Sydney I thought, *I'll go and see what this is all about*.' She was hooked at twenty.

Was it Woodbury's opening address in 1952 diagnosing Anderson's department of philosophy as a malignant growth on the mind of Sydney, or some other attraction to the diverse student body in the city, so different from her experience of student teachers in Armidale?

'It took over our lives,' she said, showing me the eleven coloured booklets from her Monday night course on Christian doctrine,

'Living the Truth,' marked in black pen with her maiden name, Mulcahy. Elizabeth was several years younger than most of the other Academy students but quickly found a few her own age, some the sisters of older students. 'We used to have dances, we used to go for picnics, sometimes with Woodbury. We'd go on the trains and the buses and the ferries because back then people didn't have cars very much. Sometimes we'd go without him and we'd just go somewhere for a bushwalk.'

Elizabeth leafed through 1952. 'AA picnic,' she read her handwritten note. 'It was an Academy picnic if it had an AA on it.'

I opened one of her albums while she put the quiche into the oven. 'I know this sort,' I called out flipping the pages of shiny black and white photographs she'd bookmarked with strips of paper. 'My grandmother had the same.' I touched the little silver triangles glued on for corners. 'They have this smell!' The same scent of sweet rubber.

'Oh, the gum,' Elizabeth came back to the dining table. 'Here we are, here's the first one,' she tapped.

'Palm Beach,' I read the caption.

'So we did one on the twenty-sixth of January, fifty-three,' she checked her diary for 1953. An Australia Day picnic while Academy classes were in recess.

'Is this you?' I peered at a young woman standing on a rock in a vintage swimming costume, one hand on her head, the other stretched toward the sea.

'Oh yeah, posing!'

I flipped over to the next bookmark.

'There's my best photo of Dr Woodbury,' she pointed at a dark shadow with a hat framed by the water. 'We were going on a ferry to Kincumber. He worked the farms. They were orphanages. Kincumber was a Catholic orphanage and Baulkham Hills was also. Same sisters.'

It was actually two different orders of sisters who ran the homes where Woodbury kept his stud farms: the Sisters of St Joseph under Mary MacKillop founded a home for boys at Kincumber and the Sisters of Mercy opened St Michael's in Baulkham Hills. Woodbury also had his cattle at another home for children and unmarried mothers at Waitara run by the Sisters of Mercy. I knew that one of Woodbury's sisters had been a Josephite. Margaret, or Auntie Maggie as the nephews and nieces called her, was three years older than Austin and entered the Mount Street convent at North Sydney in February 1917, a few months after Stephen embarked for war. Another sister, Rose, fourteen months younger than Theresa, entered the Sisters of Mercy in 1919 while Austin was in Mittagong.

Elizabeth and her friends would have been on the Kincumber ferry service from Woy Woy when the photograph was taken of Woodbury in his hat. The newest of the service fleet, the *Stella Maris*, skippered by the boys from the home, would have delivered them onto the old wharf and up the concrete steps to the sisters' sprawling property. The site is now a centre of spirituality and education with a museum, but its working farm heritage is still tangible in the dairy timber used for the Stations of the Cross that wind along the water's edge to the old boatshed and wharf. The small stable that once housed hay is now a shelter with its floor covered in clay shards and wooden beams to sit overlooking the path to the water. Perhaps the Academy picnics included a swim in the fenced-in bathing area of Brisbane Water, or a game of cricket with the older boys from the home who baked the bread rolls for Woodbury and his students.

'He was everybody's best friend,' Elizabeth said, getting the quiche out of the oven.

She discovered after his death their families were connected. 'My mother's family had all come from Mangrove,' she explained. 'And on all the documents that we've got about her family the name Woodbury comes up all the time. So his family knew my ancestors. But I didn't know at the time.'

'Did he take you up to Spencer?'

'Oh yes, I think it was his brother's house we went up to.'

'So in a way he treated you like an extended family?'

'Oh yes, it wasn't he's up there somewhere and we're all down here. It was a community.'

'It looks like a very idyllic time,' I mused out loud. Picnics by water were only a ferry ride away from the 'mad city' of Bishop Muldoon's imagination. 'We'll just have to pretend there are cows near us,' I grinned as Elizabeth handed me a warm roll with butter.

'And I learnt the most useful thing at the Academy that you could ever believe,' Elizabeth went back into the kitchen to make the tea. 'I had this white dress, just very plain white dress. I tipped my tea all over it. What do you think tea's going to do to a white dress?' she turned to ask.

'Stain it!' I knew first hand.

'Well, we had a chemist there. He said, *Quick, into the bathroom! Boiling water will take that stain out straight away.* I have always remembered if you spill tea, immediately keep it wet. The hotter the water, the better it'll get your stain out,' she carried over the full pot.

During a week bushwalking in the Blue Mountains Elizabeth and one of her Academy friends decided to holiday overseas. Both in their mid twenties at a time when young Australians were just starting to get working travel visas, they left their jobs and Academy social life to sail, bus and train their way to Vancouver, New York, London and Europe.

'We'd have wild parties,' Elizabeth's face lit up. 'A wild party consisted in turning off the lights and showing our colour slides because we'd only just started taking photographs on slides so it was a big thing!' she squealed and showed me her 1957 travel journal with decorated pages and hand-painted postcards she'd copied in water colours on the front cover.

After returning to Australia she was employed to teach first year high school students in western Sydney. Her headmaster encouraged her to get a university degree so Elizabeth enrolled in psychology at Sydney University and passed her first year using her old notes from Woodbury's lectures. She married her Italian-born husband when she was thirty-two and became a mother of five, grandmother of seven, a painter and a published composer of liturgical music. She wrote a mass, an Ave Maria that was performed in shopping centres and St Mary's cathedral, and a recessional hymn of peace that the National Council of Churches published in 2003 as part of a decade to overcome violence.

During her Academy years Elizabeth joined the choir of St Patrick's, rehearsing before lectures during the week and singing at mass on Sundays. I wondered when she had time to eat. She told me she still sings in four choirs and even travelled to Italy with one choir to sing in the Vatican, the cathedral in Florence and the basilica of Saint Francis of Assisi. Two replicas of the San Damiano cross hung on the walls of Elizabeth's kitchen and living room, the cross Franciscans venerate as the symbol of Saint Francis's vision in the chapel of San

Damiano where Christ called him to rebuild the crumbling ruins of the Catholic church.

I asked if I could hear her Ave Maria, which her choir performed in the basilica in Assisi. She got out a version sung by a Polish choir in Sydney and put it in the disc player on the floor of her living room. We sat together on her lounge underneath Saint Francis's cross and I listened with her to the female voices, then the male bass in a three-part vocal chant like an Arvo Pärt round.

'They made a few mistakes,' she said afterwards. It normally includes a fourth male tenor part. 'I was just singing along to myself in the shower one night and I thought, *I think I can write that down. That's just a scale.* My theory isn't crash hot but eventually I got it right.'

Later I listened again to Elizabeth's Ave Maria on my tape and thought of the first time I heard the Polish composer Henryk Górecki's symphony based on the prayer of an eighteen-year-old girl, Helena, held in a Gestapo prison in 1944. 'Protect me always,' Helena scratched on the wall of her cell in her own hymn for peace. The rocking sound of the last line in Polish, 'Hail Mary, full of grace,' of Górecki's soprano echoed in Elizabeth's 'Amen' of all three voices resting in one. And I thought how bread for the children was broken not at a picnic by water or city hall lecture, but in words written in the dark by a teenage girl, composed and performed in a communist state, sung in the church of Saint Francis and resounding in the living room of a high school teacher who swam in the sea and learnt a philosophy she made into her own sacred music.

5
Academicians

The ties of friendships formed in the Academy's heydays of the early fifties found Woodbury's second secretary, Joan Smith. I had seen her in Elizabeth's photos of beach outings, but after a former student rang one of her old friends from the Academy who knew Joan's number, I was having tea with a nonagenarian ex-corporal in the Women's Auxiliary Australian Air Force.

Joan made a brew of ginger tea, mentioning that her mother gave her ginger tea for menstrual pain. A shy schoolgirl from Waterloo who could never think of anything to write for essays, she told me she was good at figures and got first prize in typing in the archdiocesan commercial exam. Sister Thomas, a young Irish Sister of Mercy who taught her to type, found her an accounting job when she left school at fifteen. When Joan's father died of a brain tumour she followed her older brother into the air force and was sent to Townsville to work in cypher, passing code around the Pacific on wireless telegraphers and bunking in with twelve women in Sister Thomas's old convent, which the air force had taken over in the war.

Joan had grown up with two older brothers and relished living with 'all the girls' who went to bed, like Madeline's convent school in Paris, in nearly two straight lines: five down each side and two in the middle. She slept next to her friend she'd met on the train going up to Townsville. 'But the problem was we had no mosquito nets,' Joan said. 'It was hot and I got the most dreadful back pains, and I was thinking, *Oh God, I wish my mother was here*.' Her friend told her to go to the sick bay. 'I had dengue fever and it was a very, very bad dose I had. The back pains were dreadful.'

'Ginger tea wouldn't help that!' I laughed with her. Joan said she still keeps in touch with Mim, now ninety-two, the friend she slept next to for two years in Townsville.

Returning to Sydney to be 'de-mobbed' at the end of 1945, Joan got a job surveying radio shows while brushing up on shorthand in evening classes with Sister Philomena at St Patrick's business college, the same Sister Philomena who'd caught Patricia Woodbury at the Gestetner she'd accidentally left on during the war. Joan told Sister Philomena she was looking for work with more meaning. 'And she said, *Have you thought about joining the convent?*'

'She tried to recruit you?' Sister Philomena sounded scary.

'She had all these businessmen coming to her,' Joan said. 'They came for girls and she got them a job. She was more of a businesswoman.'

Joan said no to the convent idea, but yes to Sister Philomena's next offer to work for Woodbury for three pounds a week. Joan was twenty-three, earning five pounds a week in her radio job, and paying board to her widowed mother. Sister Philomena had contacts elsewhere so she arranged for her to work on top of the Academy job until Woodbury could pay her the extra.

'I went around for the interview,' Joan continued. 'He was puffing away like this,' she mock exhaled in her living room, 'and I said, *Do you always smoke so much?* Now I cringe, but I didn't know who he was, this philosopher, I'd never heard of what he was.'

I liked her twenty-three-year old nerve. 'Was he smoking a pipe?'

'No, cigarette, but as my husband said when he met him later, he didn't do the drawback. It was just a nervous thing in the office, not while he was teaching.'

Joan started working for Woodbury at the beginning of 1947. For the first year she supplemented her income with short-term contracts and holiday jobs at Coles, Grace Brothers, Farmers and Graziers and sorting parcels at the post office, thanks to Sister Philomena's wide business net.

'It was a barn,' Joan described the freezing office where she worked with Woodbury. He had replaced the fruit crates with chairs and put a radiator under the desk, but they had to use kerosene heaters during blackouts. 'About ten o'clock he'd say, *How 'bout a cuppa?* He'd make it. He was teaching me Latin at one stage. And I learnt to judge dairy cattle.'

Joan's dairy expertise was the result of Woodbury's second heart attack in the winter of 1953. His cleaner, Mrs Pavey, who brought him pea soup, rang the ambulance. While he was hospitalised for six weeks at the Mater, Joan had to supervise the tattooing and registering of cattle at Waitara. Lectures continued at the Academy with a Marist from the Toongabbie seminary, Wilfred Radford, stepping in for Woodbury.

The following year a wooden box of Californian chocolates was delivered to the Academy door after Joan's first dinner with the man who became her husband. His picture in his army akubra stood on her living room mantelpiece next to a photograph of Corporal Joan Smith. Woodbury married them at the end of 1955 in Joan's parish church at Waterloo where Sister Thomas had taught her to type. One of the Academy students gave them a wedding clock that sat between their photographs on the mantelpiece.

Joan had been Woodbury's secretary for nine years and he in turn became an adopted grandfather for her children, taking the older ones for walks when he visited, spoiling their appetites with sugarcoated almonds and corrupting their minds with plastic dolls.

'I used to get very annoyed with him because he'd bring out these Barbie dolls for the girls. I hated them. Imagine him going into the shop and buying them! A big fellow buying Barbie dolls.'

Her protests fell on deaf ears, but it was the dolls that taught the philosopher therapeutic play during his frequent nervous and physical ailments at the Academy.

Woodbury needed manpower as his health continued to struggle. In his mid fifties with two heart attacks behind him, he was susceptible to repeated bronchial infections and suffered like his mother from glaucoma. Laurence Fitzgerald, from the Dominican priory at Wahroonga who got his doctorate in theology from the Angelicum under Garrigou-Lagrange like Woodbury, and Colin McKay, an Irish priest with a doctorate in canon law from Maynooth seminary, were both appointed at the start of the academic year of 1955.

Radford continued to fill in for Woodbury's absences and was seconded from Toongabbie to teach full time at the Academy in 1962. Radford's appointment also spurred discussions between Woodbury and the Marist provincial, John Webber, to establish a second Academy in Parramatta and align its teaching programme with the seminary. Radford would be able to teach from Parramatta rather than commute to the city. However, Radford's appointment as rector of Toongabbie at the end of 1962 created another teaching worry for Woodbury and frustrated his plans for expansion. In November his doctor wrote to Webber recommending Woodbury take three months' complete rest from all commitments for 'nervous exhaustion'. Webber wrote to the Dominican provincial asking for reinforcements and thanking the Dominicans for their years of assistance at the Academy. Gregory Butler, an Irish-born Dominican, was sent to Woodbury's side.

Butler, like Radford before him, expressed concern for Woodbury's recurring illnesses. At the end of 1964 Butler wrote to Woodbury offering additional teaching assistance at no extra pay for the following academic year and noting the effect of Woodbury's absences on the students. 'Most of those who fell by the wayside particularly in the theology did so because they had come to hear you. Nobody takes your place,' Butler assured Woodbury, 'and with the best will in the world those who step into the breach can only do so *modo deficiati*.' Butler was forty-one and it is clear from his letter he held Woodbury in filial as well as intellectual regard as did Woodbury's students. 'Your fatherly luminous advice,' Butler finished, 'and your power of imparting the best in philosophy are assets of the highest order.'

Woodbury's influence on his students' intellectual, professional, personal and spiritual lives motivated a few men to pursue postgraduate qualifications at Catholic universities overseas in order to return as lay lecturers at the Academy. Ray Waters, a pharmacist who had been a student at the Academy since its inception and whose younger sister had travelled with Elizabeth Sancataldo on their first overseas trip, sought admission to Notre Dame University in 1956. Woodbury wrote a cover letter on his behalf to Cardinal Gilroy requesting a letter of recommendation for Waters's application. The application was apparently unsuccessful, but later he travelled to Canada with his wife, Elaine, to study at the University of Montreal and taught philosophy in Canada for over three decades before founding his own Aquinas school of philosophy for the laity.

Another student, Leo Ferrari, was bound for Quebec after being accepted into the doctoral programme for philosophy at the University of Laval. Woodbury married Leo and his wife, Kathleen

Crowley, a fellow Academy student, and there is an affectionate tone in the airmail letters Leo sent back to his former teacher to update him on his progress. In his first letter in June 1956 he told Woodbury that the lecturers were dull in comparison to the Academy, although at least his French was improving. Looking ahead already to his prospects on the academic job market he wrote, 'I am confident that if I could lecture with any resemblance to your style, I would cause a sensational revolution at any university in North America.' He sent news of Kathleen's and his growing brood of Ferraris and their faith in spite of financial pressures to continue his doctoral study. He wrote several times the following year mentioning the lack of teaching jobs and his search for employment as a chemist. After a family novena to Saint Thérèse of Lisieux he received word on Saint Thérèse's feast day of a job interview at a Jesuit university, St Mary's, in Halifax, Nova Scotia. The interview was a success and he landed his first academic job. A few years later he was teaching at an undergraduate women's college in Halifax run by the Sisters of Charity, Mount Saint Vincent. Woodbury's files include a copy of an article published by Leo Ferrari in *The Thomist* in 1961 with an inscription: 'To the beloved "Doc", who planted in my soul a love of Truth and Wisdom at the "Aquinas Academy" 1948-1955.'

Anthony Russell, an accountant who studied at the Aquinas Academy for twelve years, bypassed the cardinal and went straight to Carboni, the apostolic delegate, seeking recommendation for his application in 1958 for a doctoral programme in philosophy at the University of Montreal. Another Academy student and medical doctor, Alan Dwyer, visited Carboni in person in 1959 regarding Italian government scholarships for foreign students. Carboni wrote to Dwyer assuring him that he would follow up his request with the Catholic University of Milan and the Sacred Congregation of Seminaries and Universities in Rome.

Woodbury kept Gilroy informed about his students studying abroad. In addition to over four hundred students enrolled during the previous academic year, Woodbury reported to the cardinal at the end of 1959, one student had just completed a doctorate in Rome and was to start on a postdoctoral year at Cambridge. Another was about to commence a doctorate at Montreal and one had gained his licentiate in theology at the Institut Catholique in Paris. Several more were making arrangements to go overseas. The problem, Woodbury outlined to the cardinal the following year, was finance. The Academy could not afford to fund students to undertake doctoral study abroad. He had already written to the rector of the University of Montreal, Monsignor Irénée Lussier, about the possibility of university scholarships for Australians. He sought Gilroy's assistance in writing to Lussier to obtain Canadian government and university scholarships for Australian students to embark on doctoral programmes at Montreal. Woodbury's correspondence with both Lussier and Gilroy, reminding Gilroy that his fellow cardinal, Léger, was president of the University of Montreal, showed Woodbury's astuteness in ecclesiastical and cultural diplomacy, using his students as leverage on the ground.

The *Catholic Weekly* published regular updates on the growing numbers of Academy sons abroad, reporting Leo Ferrari's first-year doctoral results and Russell's promotion to assistant professor at Ottawa University in Canada. The newspaper told the story of a Marist brother and former student of the Academy, Ronald Fogarty, a Fulbright scholar and joint recipient of a Britannica Australia education award for his studies in educational counselling in the United States. Another student, Timothy Suttor, a lecturer in history at the Australian National University, attracted the attention of *The Australian* when he was appointed to teach theology at the University of Toronto in 1964. The newspaper said Suttor, a convert to Catholicism, had for a time joined the Dominican order before marrying and gaining his doctorate in history.

While Australians flew the flag for the Aquinas Academy in Italy, Canada and France, students at home lauded their teacher in the Academy's monthly journal, *The Academician*, which had two thousand subscribers in 1962 and three thousand on the mailing list. The editorial team of Woodbury's long-term students published articles on theology and philosophy by Woodbury as well as articles, book reviews and scatterings of verse by students, occasional lecturers and Academicians abroad. One of the editors, John Ziegler, advertised his 'Talking Thomist' classes for students to master the art of public speaking like Paddy Ryan taught in his Workers' Schools. Another editor, Don Boland, later left for Rome on 'a pilgrimage of love,' *The Academician* said, to study for a doctorate at Woodbury's old university.

The Academician was an international family with news of annual balls, Christmas parties, engagements, weddings, births and news from former students working and studying overseas. A lay missionary in Japan, Colleen English, sent back a documentary recording of Japanese songs and part of a Japanese mass for her friends from the Academy to distribute in support of her work.

Others, like Aileen Boon, who tracked down Joan Smith through her Academy networks, kept in touch with fellow Academicians for decades after, travelling together on camping trips with their families. Aileen and her younger sister attended theology classes at the Academy in the early sixties before Aileen left for London to work and travel the world for three years. Like Elizabeth Sancataldo, who had left the Academy for an overseas adventure in her mid twenties, Aileen returned to Australia and met her husband, a widower with two children under five who had lost their mother to a cerebral hemorrhage. Aileen became an instant mother at thirty-two, adding a third child in time, with wide involvement in school and family including all three sets of the children's grandparents. Aileen told me Woodbury complemented the instruction she'd received from Josephite nuns in her school, Jesuit priests in her North Sydney parish youth group and her parents, who encouraged their four daughters to form their own life choices.

'I'm just an ordinary little mum who cleans the church and cleans the brass,' Aileen said about her theology training.

I told her sometimes when I sit in church and a team of women are folding, dusting, wiping and polishing in silence, it's like meditation and I become stilled by their movements instead of irritated that women are doing God's housekeeping.

Aileen smiled. 'It's not just a building,' she responded. 'It's my prayer.'

There must have been something in the Academy water that calmed the restlessness of other newcomers, too. One student, 'E.S.,' published a poem on 'the Doctor's words' at the end of 1964, showing that not everyone fell by the wayside in Woodbury's absences, as Butler observed, but found an oasis: 'Like a shower falling on parched corn / drop after drop, refreshing wilted leaves,' was the effect of Woodbury's teaching on the 'choking dust' of this student's soul. 'Such gentle rain is not to break a drought,' ES warned other students about the slow work of recovery, yet 'thirsting land' had tasted 'a hope to put despair to rout.'

Woodbury found refreshment of his own, as he always had, in his family and farm pursuits away from the demands of teaching and public engagement. His doctor, his provincial, his teaching staff were all worried about him. His students set up a Christmas fund through *The Academician* to give him a holiday after his protracted infirmities in 1964. But even at an Academy picnic he was still on pastoral duty. Only his beloved cattle, like children at play, or the stillness of his river home, could give his mind rest and delight. One of Woodbury's nieces, Veronica, shared with me her childhood memory of riding with her uncle in the back of her father's converted Cadillac that had two benches down each side for all the children to sit on. As they drove past a field she called out to him, *Uncle Austin, look at the cows pasteurising!* He burst out laughing and she told me she never again tried to use big words to impress her famous uncle.

Veronica's younger brother, Con, became Woodbury's weekend driver in later years just as Patricia and Joan had provided companionship as well as typing in the office. Con was boarding in Sydney with his older sisters, who had attended the Academy, when their uncle rang with a rector's request.

'The Doc rang up my sister, Noreen, and said–'

Con bolted suddenly upright in his chair at the table where we were sitting in his dining room, knitting his forehead together and stilting his voice,

'–*I've got half a dozen bloody nephews in Sydney and I haven't seen one of them at the Academy.*'

Con broke down in convulsions at his strained impersonation.

'That's how he talked! So I went, and there's the Doc up the front,' Con stood up from the table and began walking around my chair, 'with his white dust coat on, and his glasses down here,' he arched his neck down toward me over his palm he pretended to read, 'he's got the book there, and the other minute he's looking at people, preaching away.'

I asked Con where he sat in class.

'Oh no matter where I sat I was a marked man!' He was still pacing around me. 'He used to come- and every time-'

Con's convulsions were infecting me.

'-he'd come over,' he inhaled sharply, 'he'd ask me a question, easy questions and I'd hardly ever get the right answer,' he burst again, 'cause I was so nervous.'

He started taking his uncle for weekend drives up the river, perhaps to cure his own nerves.

'His favourite trip was, if you go across the punt at Wiseman's Ferry, instead of turning right to go down to Spencer where he used to live, we'd go left up the hill on the old north road where it was originally built and then you'd come to a gate, and you'd open it and you could drive all the way to Wollombi.'

'Did you stop and have a picnic somewhere?'

'Oh yeah we always had a picnic and the Doc-' Con was gearing up again, 'we'd see convict roadwork-' he put on his Doc voice, '*Look at that Con!* We'd stop and look at where they'd put the stones, packed them all up to support the road and built a little bridge across the creek, little gullies, and he'd look out the window- he was always looking out for turpentine trees. Do you know what turpentine is?'

'No.'

'That's a tree that you can use to build walls in salt water. Never rots. It's the only wood that stands up to salt water and all the bugs- and he'd say, *Look at that, the turpentine down that gully Con-*'

His story ended in a coughing fit. Con's second-hand Doc made me wonder how Woodbury spoke before he went to Rome, how he said mass for his blind mother when he returned. As if his still, small voice had been displaced and so, to fill the absence, he assimilated the voices of intellectual giants in whose presence he could make his home. In its March 1967 issue *The Academician* published Woodbury's poem on the loneliness of those men who had built his favourite roads. 'The Convict's Cry' was also the cry of his own heart 'adrift and unneeded, forlorn and alone' after decades of struggling with loss and sickness: 'The daytime is empty / at night formless fears / My heart numb for aching / eyes barren of tears.'

6
A Priest and a Politician

'Julie speaking.'
'Johno Johnson.'
'Oh thank you for ringing back. I was–'
'What can I do for you?'
'Well, I was given your name by Father Michael Whelan. You contacted him through the ad in the *Catholic Weekly*? I was hoping we could arrange to meet.'
'If you come back to me with a time after the election.'
'Oh, okay. Would March the thirtieth work?'
'I said, *after the election*.'
Instinctively I felt my voice turn to wood. 'March the thirtieth is the Monday after the state election.'
'We'll still be counting then.'
'How about Wednesday the first? Will you be finished by then?'
'*After*– Julie, please. I shouldn't need to repeat this twice.'
'You mean the week after you finish counting the votes. That's the week after Easter.'
'Yes, so if you get your diary–'
'I have my diary in front of me.'
'Well I don't.'
'So what you would like is for me to call you the week after Easter, after you finish counting the votes, and then make a time?'
'Yes.'
'Fine.'
'Cheers mate,' he said before I hit End. As if I was *mates* with a bolshie, one-time state politician who once learnt philosophy from a priest twenty years before I was even *born*.

I spent the election weekend in Brisbane with a community of Marist priests I was interviewing about the Aquinas Academy. I had never been hosted by an entire group of men, let alone priests. I wondered what community life was like for vowed men who modelled themselves on Mary: men who did the hidden work of a mother. Would I be in the kitchen with them chopping vegetables before dinner?

After settling into my upstairs guest room next door to the chapel, I went down to the parlour to join Tom Ryan, John Begg and Lou Molloy for five o'clock gin. I stuck to soda water while they opened bags of chips and began to hold court from their armchairs. Tom had put the pasta bake left in the fridge by their weekday chef into the oven to warm and its aroma wafted through the dining room door.

'Here he is,' Tom announced as Jack Soulsby appeared through the screen door, singing loftily in his brown slippers. I stood up to shake his hand.

I had been looking forward to meeting Jack ever since he had recommended to me in his lyrical voice on the phone that I read London mayor Boris Johnson's *The Churchill Factor: How One Man Made History*. Jack had already told me that he came from Cornwall and had studied at the Aquinas Academy before leaving his job to become a Marist priest. I had envisaged him as a whimsical man in his mid eighties. But I hadn't imagined him so tall. Nor singing. I wondered how he had imagined me. Wearing tweed?

Jack got a glass from the cupboard, poured himself a drink and folded into place between Tom and John. I went suddenly shy while their voices seemed to fill the empty spaces as if there was a whole room of Marists present. I noticed how they called each other by name. I liked how they said mine, too, not in an effort to remember it but in the same sure way they addressed each other personally, Lou, and directly, John, mid way through, Jack, or at the end of a sentence, Tom.

'What was it like in the Depression, Lou?' came the question from Jack.

I discovered later that Jack was just a year or two younger than Lou. Like Lou, his childhood had been marked by the Great Depression and war, but on the other side of the world. Struck by such an open, unprompted enquiry, Tom, John and I turned to hear the response from one elder to another.

'I can remember, Jack, an incident when I was about three.' Lou was an engaging storyteller with an unconscious vulnerability that rose to the occasion to reveal one of his earliest memories. 'My dad lost his job so we were living in a tent outside Kempsey in South West Rocks. I was holding onto my dad's hand while he held a crab over a kerosene tin on the fire. I can still feel my hand hanging onto Dad's.'

I had to stifle a laugh at his clenched fist and eyes enormous with memory. Across the room I caught John doing the same.

'I probably didn't know what was bubbling inside the kerosene tin, but I knew I was for the crab.'

Our dinner was ready in the oven, but the crab lingered long after we left our armchairs to move to the dining table. It was part of Lou. Now I wanted to know Jack's childhood symbol.

As we climbed the stairs to Jack's study the next morning, he explained that the unopened boxes of books and half unpacked suitcases covering what would have been the living room in his unit were the remnant of an earlier move.

'How long have you been here?' I asked from behind him.

'Oh about fifteen years.'

We entered the small study and I set up the voice recorder on his desk while he cleared some space to sit among the boxes of band-aids. I recognised then the bruises all over both his arms, like my grandmother's, that the slightest bump would cause paper-thin skin to tear and bleed.

I was keen to hear about Jack's Cornish childhood. I got his birth story.

'My mother took one look at me and she said, *My God, what have I done?*'

His mother's sister, Jack's Aunt Nell, was present at the birth and kissed him 'on the botty' saying 'you will be a priest one day!' Afterwards Jack showed me his Aunt Nell's dusty prayer book stacked on a pile of books on top of the stairs.

Jack told me his father was in the British army and served in the Orkney Islands during the Second World War, leaving Jack's mother alone to raise him and his two young sisters during the Blitz.

'We were in the port of Plymouth,' Jack poked the air in front of me, pointing to Plymouth on a map he had drawn of Cornwall and Devon. 'And we went through the Blitz there, which wasn't funny.'

'How old were you? You were eight, nine?'

'It was 1941 so I was ten.'

'Ten,' I repeated.

'And, ah, I could go on and on about that.'

'Going into bunkers underground?' I tried to lift something from the musty room of memory.

'Yeah. But that's where I lost my faith.'

This I hadn't anticipated either. Tall, singing, atheist.

'I was baptised and confirmed and altar boy, processions and all that stuff. But at the age of ten when I saw those bombers coming over and I knew they were trying to bomb the mother that I loved and my two sisters, I said, *There's no God*. And that began a period of almost twenty years for me without a God.'

'Your mother must have been heartbroken,' I steered the conversation back to his mother protecting her children in a war.

'Well, yes and no. She'd lapsed from the church, but she made sure that we went to mass.'

'Was your father Catholic as well?'

'Yeah. But he was non-practicing and, you know, the thinking in those days for many people was get the child baptised and confirmed and that's it. You go to mass,' he wiggled his finger like a parent, 'and then come back and tell me what the priest said. And sometimes I'd skip mass and then I had to invent a sermon.'

I could imagine that. 'She'd have worked that out pretty quick!'

'My mother was very close to me. She still is. She's up in heaven now. But that's very close.'

I laughed and Jack patted his chest. 'Really it is. It's in here,' he said and then started to sing, 'The bird with feathers of blue is waiting for you back in your own backyard–'

'Where does that singing come from?' Jack's musical box was putting a spell on me.

'My father played the banjo and ukulele. But you could tell how close the bombs were coming by the noise.'

We were back in the Blitz. The bombs were as close to his heart as his mother.

'Plymouth was a military target,' he began. 'Ships galore and bombers galore and we were on the edge of it. When a bomber turns and he's dropped half his load and he's coming back, he'd never take the bombs back home so they'd drop them anywhere. If it was low-key you didn't bother to go to the shelter. But if it was really loud and close,' he left his sentence unfinished.

'This bomb was coming pretty close and I can still see it to this day. My mother threw my sister and I under the—she was carrying a baby at the time—she threw my sister and I under the table. She threw her body on top of us. So you had the floor, kids, mum, table,' his hand split the air horizontally on each word, 'and then the bomb fell, but not on us, about three or four doors up. And all that happened to us was incendiaries on the roof,' he paused, 'and shattered glass.'

It was the first time I had heard Jack pause. 'That happened many times, actually,' he spoke again. 'But I've never forgotten what my mother was prepared to do for me.'

Like Lou's crab, the bird with blue feathers was part of Jack.

When I got back from Brisbane I listened to a Billie Holiday recording of Jack's song. 'Oh you can go to the East / go to the West / but someday you'll come / weary at heart / back where you started from / you'll find your happiness lies / right under your eyes / back in your own backyard.'

What brought Jack back, twenty years and a migrant passage to Australia later, to the faith he lost underneath his mother? Back to the words his Aunt Nell planted in a prophetic peck on his baby 'botty'? What made him sing again after the bombs?

'Johno, this is Julie. We spoke before Easter. The Aquinas Academy. About a time to meet?'

'I'm in a cab. Diary's at work. Be there in an hour.'

I sent some emails. Drank tea.

'It's Julie again. Can we make a time now?'

'Diary's on my desk.' Muffled sounds. I heard Johno say 'righto' to someone. Shuffling paper.

'How is Thursday the sixteenth of April?' I asked as he came back on the phone. 'Or the following week?'

'Wait a minute, love. The sixteenth. That's a lot of pages.' More shuffling. 'Right, the sixteenth is free.'

'Great. I can come and meet you. Are you in the city?'

'We're at three-seven-seven Sussex Street. Ninth floor. Ring on approach. Meet in the foyer. Eleven o'clock.'

'Johno, I'm on the ninth floor.'

'I said, *Ring on approach*. I'm down in the lobby.'

Julie, Juuuliie. I spun to the echo of my name in the empty lobby where a few minutes earlier I had sped through to the lift. *Julie!* I spun back to the mirrored lift, then to the empty lobby again, and finally peered toward the pot plant in the corner by the automatic doors.

'Johno?' A hunched shadow outlined the green foliage like Orson Welles out of *The Third Man*.

'Just finishing this off,' he flicked the cigarette stub in his fingers into the pot as I came around the talking leaves.

The shadow looked up from under a dark grey hat with a yellow feather like a cockatoo crest.

'You ran straight past me.'

I decided to sit down on the other side of the pot and keep listening to the leaves. They told me they had retired and came in every day to do volunteer work. They also said they had belonged to the Party for sixty-six years.

I thought of Sister Patricia, a Dominican for sixty-seven.

After more leaf talk about party personalities and passing 'hi Johnos' from anyone who walked through the automatic doors, we stood up with Johno's two walking sticks and made our way together past the lifts to the stairs down to the coffee stand in the old Trades Hall.

'Always bloody broken.' Johno pointed his stick at the wheelchair lift and the technician trying to repair it. I ordered flat whites and friends while Johno chose a corner table, after telling a nearby pair of business-shirted patrons they should pay rent for their regular meeting.

I had already looked up Johno's parliamentary record and read his maiden speech in the New South Wales upper house in which he named the four nuns who taught him in high school: Sisters Mary

Kieran, Aiden, Koska and Mary de Sales Daly of the Presentation Order in Lismore. I wanted to start with the women who gave him an education.

'I had nine weeks in high school. Note that. My total schooling.'

'But you would have gone to the local state primary school?' I asked.

'Don't guess. I keep telling my kids that. Don't ask a question and then answer it,' he wheezed a hee-hee-hee as if it was a game.

'Okay,' I played along. 'Did you go to a state primary school, Johno?'

'No, I went to a Catholic school.'

Before he turned ten, while attending the local Catholic primary school in his hometown of Murwillumbah, he broke his arm and contracted tetanus. He showed me the scar on his right forearm where the bone had come through. He was sent to Brisbane because it was the only hospital in the region that accepted tetanus patients.

'And I can remember I was in a room that had very dark, velvet curtains,' Johno said.

The plaster left him with a clawed right hand and he left high school early because of the months he had missed in primary school with tetanus. But he received some parting words from the nuns in Lismore.

'One of them said, *When you leave school always remember this: go to mass on Sunday, marry a Catholic, join your trade union, bank Commonwealth and vote Labor.* And I can give them all a tick.'

After leaving high school in 1945, Johno worked in a retail store in Murwillumbah before landing a Christmas mail job in Sydney in 1954. On the last day before he was due to leave Sydney he ran into a school friend who offered him a job at Anthony Hordern's department store. 'And on my first pay day I walked over here and joined my trade union.'

He rose through the ranks of the shop assistants' union and was elected member of the Legislative Council for twenty-five years and president for thirteen. When Johno retired in 2001, the state deputy opposition leader paid tribute to the parliamentary prayer group he led each week in his presidential suite with colleagues of different creeds. But my purpose for meeting Johno was neither his religious nor his political creed, though his line that he took his religion from Rome and his politics from Sussex Street was punchy. Later I discovered it underlined in an article Johno gave me on Cardinal Moran who said 'home' instead of Sussex Street. Moran had taken it from Daniel O'Connell, the Irish emancipation leader, a century before.

I wanted to know how a Rome-educated philosopher, Father Austin Woodbury of the Aquinas Academy, whom Johno acknowledged along with the Presentation sisters in his outgoing parliamentary speech, had such a profound impact on a young trade unionist who didn't finish high school. He could have become a priest like Jack Soulsby if a vocation to politics hadn't won out.

I was starting to see some patterns. Jack survived the bombs but lost his faith. Johno survived tetanus but lost his chance for further education. Both owed their lives to strong-minded women. And both revered Austin Woodbury as their spiritual father.

Jack was fourteen when his father came home from the war. His father's sister, who lived in Australia, invited the family out so while Jack completed his Cambridge School Certificate his father left the family again to come to Sydney. Then seventeen-year-old Jack, his mother and two younger sisters followed him on the *Ormonde.*

Six years after bringing his family out to Australia, Jack's young father died of lung cancer. Jack was twenty-three. He had been working as a cadet engineer for Gutteridge, Haskins and Davey in Castlereagh Street while studying at night for an engineering diploma. His devout Catholic boss, Geoffrey Innis Davey, who had stood as a Liberal for the federal seat of Hume, made a lasting impression on Jack. His black and white portrait on Jack's bookshelf eyeballed Jack at his desk while we talked in his study. One day Jack went into Davey's library, found a book on Catholic social teaching called *The Framework of a Christian State*, took it home on the train and stayed up all night reading it. Three lines he could still recite by heart floored him.

'Man-woman,' he added, 'has a certain nature within them and from that nature, once they've discovered it, spring the rights they can enjoy and the duties they must carry out.'

Jack was on a roll addressing me then Davey on the bookshelf.

'You have to understand,' he turned back to me, 'this immature kid coming out of England felt that he existed only by courtesy of the English government and the German government, who did their best to kill him, and then the Aussie government who accepted him as a migrant. So I lived and I breathed courtesy of them and my value depended on what those governments thought of me. And they could change their mind tomorrow if they wanted.'

I asked Jack if his father's death had any impact on his discovery.

'Oh, it's all interrelated.' He said it again as if he hadn't made the link.

Jack was twenty-seven when he had his epiphany that there was something more in the universe than engineering. He was, as he put it, 'half formed.'

I nodded.

'You know what I'm talking about.'

I did. 'It's like having one arm longer than the other arm.'

'Yeah. One leg longer than the other.' He got carried away. 'One ear and one eye and one top lip.'

Except I was a few years older than Jack when I realised I was living in an academic hothouse, swapping continents and pretending to myself and everyone else it was my natural home. I joined a painting studio. Jack went into amateur theatre. He started going to mass. Then he saw an ad about the Aquinas Academy in a copy of the *Catholic Weekly* he had picked up in church.

> There comes a point in life if you are lucky, when you are old, or if you are even luckier, when you are young, when you ask yourself questions and begin to seek for the answers.

Perhaps it was these three lines that jumped out at Jack after he pinched Davey's book and began to strut Sydney's stages. He'd have read on:

> In the lecture hall of the Aquinas Academy at 152 Gloucester Street each weekday evening the questions in the minds of all sorts of people are being answered by Dr A.M. Woodbury and his staff of lecturers and tutors.

From Jack's office in Castlereagh Street it was a mile's walk four evenings a week for five years down Hunter and George to The Rocks where he got 'drunk every night' on metaphysics.

'Like milk?' I asked.

'Like whiskey.'

One evening in class Jack heard a voice say, 'I want you to be like the bloke up the front.'

'I nearly fell off my chair,' Jack told me. 'How can I do that?'

The voice answered. 'Plant yourself in the same soil.'

So Jack Soulsby, the kid from Cornwall whose mother saved him from the bombs, entered the Marist seminary at Toongabbie at the age of thirty-three. Jack had to give up his engineering salary, which supported his widowed mother. Five years later she attended his ordination in a wheelchair with terminal lung cancer. She died the mother of a priest she had protected with her own body.

Johno read the *Catholic Weekly*, too. He signed up for the next term's classes at the Aquinas Academy as quick as he'd joined his trade union the day he banked his first paycheck. He began reading papal social encyclicals: *Rerum novarum* ('Of revolutionary change') published a few months before the Labor Party was founded in 1891 – Johno and I both smiled at that papal joke – and *Quadragesimo anno* forty years later condemning both capitalism and communism and pointing a Roman finger at parties who used the word 'Christian' for their fascist politics.

Johno moved in with four other Academicians in Ashfield. Each Sunday they spent their afternoons standing on wooden boxes in the Domain baiting Communists and Protestants. They went on to Park Street in the evening, caught the tram to Kings Cross, set up another box, and continued into the night. Johno was still spitting at 'Comms,' and Labor 'lunatics' who had expelled their own party members, as if he had climbed up on his chair with his walking stick to thump the table in Trades Hall.

When I asked about his papal knighthood he told me to ring Rome. If I was guessing I'd say it was for his service on the board of *Catholic Weekly*, but when I asked if it was for his political service he thumped the table again.

'The church does not take part in politics.'

'Well not officially,' I replied evenly. Although I wasn't about to climb onto my chair to thump the point, I wanted to say that *yes* papal social teaching had distinguished between Catholics acting under spiritual authority of their bishops, and Catholics acting on their own political initiative in a party or trade union or dissident movement; and *no* it was a muddy slope. In Rome and at home.

'It does not take part in politics,' Johno repeated. 'You could be a bride today and a widow tomorrow if the pendulum swings.'

We swung back instead to two of Johno's anti-communist heroes: Lech Walesa, the Polish electrician jailed for leading non-violent shipyard strikes as leader of the independent trade union, Solidarity, who later received the Nobel Peace Prize; and Karol Wojtyla, who became John Paul II the year I was born.

'Walesa was a man after your heart,' I told Johno.

'He was indeed. The trade union movement under the auspices of the shop assistants' union raised enormous amounts of money for Solidarity. A retired doctor at Rose Bay who owned a private hospital in Wollongong, instead of selling it closed it down and sent all of the equipment to Lech Walesa.'

'He was embarrassing to some on the left,' I responded. 'A dissident trade union leader saying the rosary with his family.' I hadn't realised there had been such a huge international fundraising effort for Solidarity.

'I'll never forget this moustached shipyard worker being hurled over the gates of the Gdansk shipyard. The free city of Gdansk,' Johno said.

The Polish pope got a mention in his outgoing parliamentary speech, but it was Austin Woodbury's name that entered Johno's hall of fame along with the Lismore nuns. He'd had nine weeks with the nuns and six years with 'the Doc', yet Johno seemed at a loss to weigh up his legacy apart from a few pithy Woodbury lines. The trade unionist from Speaker's Corner and president of the Legislative Council was stumped for words.

'It developed me.' He slumped back in his seat. 'I remember him saying,' Johno sat up again to quote his mentor, '*God who is infinitely good in himself, would not permit evil were the good to come therefrom.*'

I asked if Woodbury's teaching had supplemented the high school education Johno missed out on. Long pause. Sip of coffee.

'Well you could ask any student of the university,' he put his cup back on its saucer, 'what's your outcome? Your outcome is you're an engineer or a solicitor.' Johno sat next to law and engineering students who attended the evening classes. It was an Academy for all educations.

'The Aquinas Academy put a stamp on me,' he said in the end. 'I can defend the church on all issues.'

He was back on his box. I was unconvinced. Both Jack and Johno relayed stories of Woodbury's antics in the classroom that were funny, but didn't explain his magnetic hold. Jack's impersonation of a snorting bull at a red rag in full exegetical flight and Johno's clawed hand and 'bugger thats' imitating the absent-minded philosopher who forgot to pick up the chalk when he went to write on the board, convinced me Woodbury was an electric teacher. Like Con Woodbury's dining room show of his uncle, Jack and Johno made me laugh and wonder at the same time at the power of performance. I could piece together a hundred more anecdotes from 'the Doc's' devotees, but the lines would still keep blurring his face.

Probably he'd tell me off again for guessing, but the velvet darkness of Johno's childhood hospital room seemed a potent symbol of what he found in the face of a man he looked up to all his adult life. That face was lined with shock, sickness, sadness, loneliness and anxiety. It was a face that could make Jack's bombs fall still. Whatever Johno and Jack saw in the face of Austin Woodbury, even if only a momentary glow, was drawn in the dark.

7
Seeing in the Dark

'How would you describe dusk to a blind person?' the teacher asked.

We were seated in front of our easels on low wooden stools in the studio drinking tea and listening to the painter, John Ogburn, talk about the difference between seeing and knowing. Nearly seventy years earlier he had learnt to see in Woodbury's philosophy classes. Now John's students were sharing insights from their teacher who taught them to see in paint.

I was sitting next to Margaret Craw, who told me that the question about dusk had stuck in her mind ever since she came to John's studio in the early seventies as a young art school graduate from Brisbane. Marita Brahe, John's widow and my painting teacher, was playing us a tape from one of John's classes in 1984. As I listened to his quick-paced words, I thought of Woodbury's blind mother writing to her son, Jack Soulsby's blackout bombs and my own reluctance to see something in lit fragments.

When I first arrived at the studio with my beginners' set of Reeves' oil paints two years after John had died, Marita told me John had studied philosophy under Woodbury in the late forties before becoming a Catholic. It was the first time I had heard of the Aquinas Academy or its Marist founder. Much later amongst Woodbury's correspondence I came across a letter from John Ogburn on three cream artist's folio sheets with black inkblots in the margins of his large handwriting. Woodbury had invited Ogburn to the Academy's silver jubilee celebrations in 1970. He couldn't make it but wrote instead a flowing tribute to his former teacher who kept the letter, as the Austrian poet, Rainer Maria Rilke, might have described it, as a 'thing' with its own 'thereness,' like a letter Rilke himself might have written in copperplate on blue paper.

'I always think of the Aquinas Academy as your spouse and my alma mater,' wrote Ogburn to Woodbury. 'Many children must have been borne of this union. The food you served for the main dish was Truth but you have the genius for serving delightful and invigorating appetisers and thoughtful liquers. You and your spouse were certainly the most direct cause in leading me to seek the source of Love and Truth and finding its richest expression in Holy Mother Church.'

Ogburn was twenty-two, had left his job as an industrial chemist and was working as a freelance journalist for the *Sydney Morning Herald* when he was introduced to Woodbury. He went along, as he put it later writing about his early life, to 'have some fun with these spooky medievalists.' At the same time that he began attending evening classes at the Academy, he started painting and drawing classes with the Hungarian Jewish painter, Desiderius Orban, a member of The Eight group of Hungarian modernists influenced by French post-impressionism. Orban had established a studio in Circular Quay after fleeing Budapest in the war. For Ogburn, the twin pursuits of philosophy and painting 'gradually opened my eyes so I began to see.'

Childhood loss, for John Ogburn the painter as for Jack Soulsby the priest and Johno Johnson the politician, was a thread in common with Woodbury's own past. Ogburn viewed his childhood in northwestern Victoria through a palette of literal and metaphoric darkness after his mother died when he was three and his father remarried a woman whom Ogburn remembered for her acts of cruelty, locking him in a closet under the stairs as punishment for misdeeds. Yet there were also moments of what he referred to as 'a ravishing loveliness.' He described one such experience outside Ballarat, a place called 'The Gong' he visited at the age of about ten with his father and stepmother on the way to pick up his older sisters from boarding school. 'There were forms of various kinds, a small creek of clear water dancing over white quartz pebbles, a secluded place. No doubt a micro-climate, a miniature rain forest. Suddenly, without any warning, I burst into tears. I tried to avoid being seen,' Ogburn recalled, but 'it was the sheer loveliness of the place that moved me so much.'

His Anglican father sent him to board at Caulfield grammar school in Melbourne where Ogburn grew into a religious skeptic, refusing to kneel before a piece of bread in communion. He became an orphan when his father died during his final year at high school and he turned to the 'hard reason and cold facts' of science, eventually working for Shell petroleum and dabbling in weekend painting and drawing until his encounter with Orban convinced him art could be an intellectual occupation.

Woodbury's command of the classroom and direct method of questioning, which awed and terrified some students, impressed Ogburn who had a few questions of his own. Transubstantiation, for one. 'He delighted in being questioned,' Ogburn said. 'Woodbury would send me to the canvas with his answer and then stick the boot in a couple of times to make sure. I responded to this as a miner greets the fresh air after working a double shift underground.' Drilling a luminous depth that had first ravished his ten-year-old vision, Ogburn found at last 'the source of that clear stream of loveliness and beauty, the Being from which or in which all other beings are. I could now start to paint seriously.'

Ogburn's religious skepticism had not completely dissipated. He wrote to CS Lewis in a state of desperation, as he described it, 'to avoid bowing to Rome.' He wanted to know why Lewis had joined the English and not the Roman church on his return to Christianity. Lewis replied that he had returned to 'mere Christianity,' a term Ogburn grew eventually to understand as his own 'primitive' practice of faith. At twenty-four he was received into the Catholic church by a Jesuit priest, Father Michael Scott, who gave Ogburn a job teaching art at Campion Hall in Point Piper, a boys' preparatory school for St Ignatius' college. He began exhibiting his paintings before a stint abroad to study European art.

I wondered if Woodbury visited his student's first solo exhibition at the Macquarie Galleries in Sydney in 1953. In Europe in his late twenties Woodbury had studied the Renaissance masters, the 'immaterial loveliness' of Fra Angelico, the stained glass of Chartres. Ogburn, too, was taken by Chartres in the first flush of his Catholic faith, approaching the cathedral 'through the wheat fields to the south, the tips of the spires appearing first like the masts of a ship in a sea of ripening wheat.'

But Woodbury remained a Renaissance man, commissioning a local artist, Barbara Hearn, to paint a portrait of Saint Thomas

Aquinas using the friars in their Dominican habits at the Wahroonga priory as models for her subject. The *Daily Mirror* art columnist described Hearn's painting, her first work in oil, as 'one of the most arresting and accomplished works of art to be seen in Sydney for many a long day.' The canvas, which hung on public display in EJ Dwyer's Catholic emporium in George Street after its unveiling by Cardinal Gilroy in March 1953, 'is a forceful and striking study of a commanding personality, carried out with a great deal of imagination and technical skill.' The face of Saint Thomas, according to the art critic who might also have been Woodbury's student, 'is virile and alive with intelligence and spiritual fervour.' Woodbury declared it to be superior even to well-known depictions of the saint by Lippi, Zurbarán and Ghirlandaio. Colour replicas were sold to raise funds for the Academy where the painting eventually hung in the lecture hall.

Hearn's painting now hangs in the main lecture theatre of Campion College, a Catholic liberal arts campus in the former Toongabbie seminary that Woodbury founded. Thomas Aquinas, the patron saint of university students, looks out over the purple seats of the lecture theatre from his wooden chair, sandalled feet planted on a circle of stone with his left foot raised on a platform above his right. Behind his left shoulder is a stone arch that leads down a dark cloister to a window, perhaps a cell where he wrote his *Summa theologiae*. The cracks in the paint show through the wood of the chair and the black *cappa magna* of his Dominican habit, but the light Hearn painted on his face the way iconographers illuminate divine grace in their subjects is still uncracked. Opposite him is a copy of a Byzantine icon of Mary, *Salus Populi Romani*, with her own dark cape of protection holding her child who looks at her and points with his right hand to the cross on her mantle. Both the painting and the icon are the art of devotion, its subject and viewer locked in mutual gaze.

For Ogburn unlike Woodbury, the art of presence and being was a living experience that didn't end with the Renaissance or the Romantics, but passed into the modern works of Cézanne and Matisse. Matisse's works were among those the Nazi state deemed 'degenerate' and seized from German museums and private art collections in 1937. Ogburn's teacher, Orban, also had his *Cathedral in Eger* seized from the Nuremberg Museum. Ogburn's debt to Matisse, who died in France while Ogburn was living in London, was as transformative as his encounter with the sixth-century mosaic of the transfiguration in the Basilica of Sant'Apollinare outside Ravenna, an experience he described as being 'bathed in the coolness of the green, white and gold of the mosaic, as fresh as though the tesserae were laid yesterday, as solemn as though made by the disciples themselves.'

Bathing in sixth-century green tiles, like the freshness of a Matisse nude with oranges, which hangs next to the mounted row of wooden easels in the corner of John Ogburn's studio, is the art of presence and being. This is what Ogburn set out to create in his still lives and cloth-draped interiors. 'The colour arabesques of the crocheted, embroidered, woven draperies envelop the objects as a pulsating field of energy, filling the atmosphere with a seething current of colour,' wrote a Hungarian art historian after an exhibition of Ogburn's work in Budapest, the home of his teacher, Orban.

On return to Sydney Ogburn taught philosophy of painting at the Christian Brothers' training college at Strathfield and Mulgoa, instructing novices in the art of seeing rather than any method or theory. He also taught at Orban's studio before opening his own studio. One former Christian Brother, Graham English, who had learnt to see in Ogburn's classes for novices in the early sixties, continued painting in Ogburn's studio until the late seventies and after leaving the order. I visited Graham and his wife, Erin White, in their home covered with both John's and Graham's works, some with religious motifs: John's ink drawing of Christ's agony in the garden and Graham's painting of a priest facing the altar before the Second Vatican Council turned the priest around to face the people.

Ogburn's belief in the independence of art from both dealer and critic led him to found a co-operative gallery run by artists free from government and commercial constraints. The Harrington Street Gallery, now in its Chippendale location after the studio and gallery moved out of The Rocks, is a contemplative place of 'un-clamorous' art, as the American art critic, Clement Greenberg, wrote after visiting. A place where Ross Coady's *Dawn Haiku*, blushed in spare pale pink and gold, bears witness to a deep and fragile longing, Peter Carr's spinach leaves in an earthen vessel name themselves on the canvas, Margaret Craw's *Secure* enfolds a baby's crown in the flesh strokes of its mother, and John Ogburn's *Australian Bobby Dazzler* sky swims in honeycomb light.

I took John's question on a tour for blind and vision-impaired visitors of the Art Gallery of New South Wales' new Matisse acquisition, *Jazz*. I joined a young woman with a doctorate in art, a grandmother in a wheelchair with her carer and a woman with dark glasses and her guide dog on the tour that took in some of the gallery's modern collection. First we studied the geometric shapes of Cézanne's *Banks of the Marne*, the green orb of a tree canopy shading the lime-washed rectangles of the village walls like the travertine tiles we had walked across in the gallery forecourt and the young woman had tapped with her white stick to sound the acoustic stone.

'What's the colour of the water?' the grandmother asked our guide, who described its splotches of reflected green riverbank, cream and caramel walls, red triangle roofs and patchwork blue clouds. Her answer reminded me of James McBride's memoir of his Jewish mother who told him, one of her twelve black children, that God was the colour of water. *Water doesn't have a colour*, his mother said. Then our guide showed us Cézanne's pixellated lines of paint brushing soft downward strokes side by side with her finger on the tops of our hands.

We moved to Picasso and I sat on a fold-up stool staring at the bamboo tiles under my shoes trying to imagine his nude in a rocking chair with her head like a backwards 'D.' Gradually I began to see the raw coarse canvas of her skin and thick brown strokes of the Bentwood frame incised with the end of a brush like a scored rim of pie. The blood red flowed below her oversized crossed bare feet like an open gash on the floor.

I had paid close attention when our guide told us Matisse created his *Jazz* series of coloured stencils with scissors after surgery for colon cancer left him in a wheelchair. But I hadn't noticed the dimmed lighting as we moved from the oil paintings of Cézanne and Picasso to Matisse's works on paper behind glass until the woman wearing dark glasses asked what the light was like. The layer on layer of visual description was wearing me down after less than an hour. I focused on the black, pink and white spirals of seaweed swirling around a blue and green lagoon, a white arabesque figure floating diagonally across two black boxes with a blue and green border called *The swimmer in the tank*, the grey behind black behind pink behind white behind red heart like a Russian paper doll, the Matisse orange I remembered from the print in John's studio. While the others closed in to trace what they could see through the glass with their finger, I thought of Bishop Muldoon's 'mad city' as I read with my full vision the quote on the gallery wall by Matisse who said in 1947 of his paper cut-outs: 'The hand is only an extension of sensibility and intelligence. [...] My curves are not mad.'

The moral, aesthetic, intellectual, social, political and economic danger of our day, John Ogburn stated in his talk as I listened on the wooden studio stool, the 'original problem' that has existed since Adam and Eve, is the desire to know without seeing. The voice of the critic, the tempter in the garden, says, *You can know without seeing*. It is the critical voice that turns knowledge into 'puffed up answers of what someone else has seen,' John said. But God can't be proved any more than Rembrandt can, he went on, and I wondered what his philosophy teacher would say to that. God, or Rembrandt – or Matisse, for that matter—can only be witnessed. To give true witness to what I alone see, what no one else sees, to say *I have seen* or *I have not seen*, is life's creative purpose, John finished.

Later when I wrote up my notes from John's talk I heard their echo in words I had copied earlier by the French philosopher, Jean-Louis Chrétien, in *The Ark of Speech* where speech is both wound and witness arising from silence. 'It is, like love, irreplaceable, and nothing can stand in for it; no other work can replace this speech, and nobody can replace us in this speech. Anyone who has asked another to love in their place would not love. Anyone who has asked another to give thanks in their place would not be giving thanks. This speech has the strength of its weakness, for the voice that praises always has something tremulous about it, knowing at one and the same time that it cannot be enough and yet that nothing other than it *can* be enough.' It is the sensible and intelligent hand of Matisse sculpting colour with scissors in a wheelchair when he could no longer paint with a brush at an easel.

'In our common Father, the Good, the True and The Beautiful,' John Ogburn signed his letter to Woodbury. For Ogburn in the end, beauty, truth and goodness were not dogmatic schema that could be proved, though he never lost his Catholic faith for which he owed a debt to Woodbury, his first teacher in the faith. 'The Church in teaching, if not always in practice, of the transcendent reality of Beauty has allowed me to remain calm, and given me the certainty I needed to develop my art independent from, and unfortunately of necessity, mostly outside the comfortable bounds of the prevailing fashions,' he wrote forty years after his confirmation in the Catholic church. John's hope, to which he bore witness through painting and teaching others to see, of 'being born again into a world of never ending ravishing loveliness is my joy, my meaning.'

If I had to answer John's question about seeing in the dark, I would say that it is also a sacramental witness. The creative act of bearing witness is to name what is beyond sight but close enough to touch. It is to show what I have seen, what no one else has seen in my place. This is what I saw:

Moonrise at Dusk. Marita Brahe. Oil on canvas.

> Leaving all you once held near,
> you slip under
> an eiderdown of mauve, indigo
> and alizarin brushing over
> your beautiful light
> that is not lost, but is only asleep
> below the milk-still moon
> who stays upstairs like a face
> all night.
>   As if this
> arc of earth caressed
> by evening benediction
> bears witness to the day ended
> in a flock of burnt orange, ochre
> and viridian saying *Yes*
> to all that is yet to come.

8
Going To Rome

Sister Hildebrand Russell from the Benedictine abbey of New Norcia wrote to Woodbury at the beginning of 1960 to thank him for his philosophy texts he had sent for her novices. She told him she would remember 'the great apostolate you are carrying on' in her prayers. Like a Thomist missionary, Sister Hildebrand was taking Woodbury's apostolate to the Benedictine novitiate across the other side of the continent.

A Vincentian priest in Ashfield, John Robinson, also expressed his gratitude for Woodbury's teaching. 'I was delighted, edified, and enlightened,' Robinson wrote, 'first at the subject matter delivered and secondly at the masterful manner of delivery. I have learned to a great extent what to preach, but more especially how to preach, that is, from top to toe. I learned as much with my eyes as with my ears,' he said. 'In the intellectual world a great light beams forth from 152 Gloucester Street continually. Before long it will be seen by everyone.'

Notes of appreciation from a nun instructing novices in New Norcia and a priest learning the art of preaching in a Sydney parish, like a letter from a painter teaching his own students to see, were not mere trophies in Woodbury's cabinet of success stories. They were strategic assets in the business of creating a Catholic university in Australia that could shine its own light amongst the rest of the world's luminary Catholic universities.

Rome's approval required more than papal medals. Woodbury looked to his long time champion, Daniel Hurley, who wrote to Woodbury from Rome's headquarters of the Society of Mary in 1952: 'Father General is very interested in the prospect of Pontifical recognition. Surely, it must come.' In August 1954 Woodbury informed Hurley and the Australian provincial, James Harcombe, of his recent visit to the apostolic delegate, Carboni. 'The gist of it is this,' Woodbury got to the point. 'The Holy See is desirous of proceeding at once to the establishment of either a Catholic University or of an Institute of Philosophy and of Theology of Pontifical status in Sydney (but national, I understand, not diocesan),' he added. If the idea of a Catholic university went ahead, the Aquinas Academy would become a faculty of philosophy in its own right. If the second option of a pontifical institute eventuated instead, then the Academy would have full accreditation from Rome to confer degrees in philosophy and theology taught by an academic cohort, including priests and religious, with doctoral expertise in philosophy, theology or law. Woodbury would have 'complete direction' over the curriculum and supervision of lecturers with the support of the cardinal, which Woodbury took to mean in financial terms. He urged Hurley and Harcombe to authorise the proposal, he ended, 'fulfilling the aims with which the Aquinas Academy was inaugurated,' the aims which Woodbury himself had first proposed to Hurley in New Zealand. 'This is a greater thing than a diocese,' Woodbury relayed Carboni's words to his Marist superiors.

Harcombe was on his way to Rome for the Marist general chapter when Woodbury's letter arrived. He replied that he would take up the matter on behalf of the superior general in person with Carboni on his return to Sydney. Woodbury was not used to being told to sit tight. Hurley, to soften the blow, encouraged him in the meantime to seek out the finer points of finance from Carboni. The Society of Mary could not afford to fund the scheme, 'that, I feel sure, would be understood by the Cardinal and the Delegate,' he told Woodbury.

Rome acted discretely. A letter to Carboni in September 1954 from Cardinal Pizzardo, prefect of the Sacred Congregation of Seminaries and Universities that had authority to confer pontifical status on Catholic institutes of higher education, expressed 'the most intense wishes that the unceasing efforts of His Eminence the Cardinal Archbishop of Sydney to endow Australia with a Catholic University of vast and powerful radiation may have a most happy success within the temporal limits he has in mind.' The matter was over. Rome had spoken. The university was Gilroy's domain, not Woodbury's. Woodbury kept the letter on file, presumably in his own translation from the original Latin, which Carboni must have handed to him with a wordless shrug. The apostolic delegate could grace the annual Academy inaugurations with glowing tributes to its rector, but he could not make Woodbury's dream come true. Nor could Hurley, who returned to Sydney the following year to take up duties again as parish priest at St Patrick's.

The pontifical title for a school of theology went instead to St Patrick's seminary at Manly. Muldoon was made dean until his appointment as auxiliary bishop in 1960. Muldoon's plans for expanding the Academy's work in the 'mad city' became another strategic asset in Woodbury's academic enterprise that included a second campus at Parramatta as an extension of the Toongabbie seminary. When Woodbury's plan fell through at the end of 1962, he turned to the Dominicans for help in Rome.

One of Woodbury's old lecturers at the Angelicum, the former Irish Dominican master general, Michael Browne, had just been made cardinal. Another Irish-born Dominican from the Wahroonga priory, Reginald Batten, had taught at the Academy for five years, replacing Lawrence Fitzgerald before him, until his transfer to Canberra and replacement with Gregory Butler. Batten wrote to Browne in October 1962 about the pontifical prospects for the Academy. He mentioned the total enrollment of between six and seven hundred students in 1962 and the growing numbers of Academicians working towards doctorates overseas including one, Geoff Deegan, who had recently left Sydney to begin a doctorate at the Angelicum.

'The intellectual situation of Australian Catholics is not at all as healthy as some like to think it is,' Batten informed Browne. Catholics occupying academic posts had taken degrees in the world's most prestigious institutions: Oxford and Cambridge. The problem with their privileged education was their disregard for and prejudice against Thomism. 'Instead, eclecticism, Oxford-style linguistic analysis, Wittgenstein, etc., are some of the prevailing influences.' Moreover, even practicing Catholics felt free to dispense with the church's teaching in papal encyclicals. 'The danger is doubly great,' Batten continued, when 'Catholic intellectuals, having just recently been admitted to academic circles, are anxious to conform, as far as possible, to the prevailing pattern, to "go along" with non-Catholics as far as it can be done.' Enter the Aquinas Academy, which for the past seventeen years 'has been the only real bulwark of Catholic thought here, and, as I know for a fact, has saved many a student's faith from shipwreck.' Confidentially, Batten mentioned to the cardinal, 'many of us at the Academy, both staff and pupils, look forward to the day when it may be possible to see this institution raised to the status of a Pontifical Academy. Many more, especially the teaching nuns and brothers, would attend if this were so.'

Batten received a reply eight months later, delayed no doubt by Browne's attendance at the Second Vatican Council and the death of Pope John XXIII at the beginning of June. His reply to Batten was dated 18 June 1963, the day before he entered the papal enclave to elect Paul VI. 'My dear Father Reginald,' he wrote, 'nothing could be better in intellectual work for sound thought within the Church than the ideal of the Aquinas Academy. Moreover, thought is rampant on many fields, and there is no possibility of Thomism ever becoming outmoded, whether as a philosophical foundation or as a remedy against the errors of the day.' Browne's defence of Thomism in the midst of the council's deliberations about the future of theological training signalled his caution at the 'new Pentecost' that John XXIII had foreseen in the council's work. 'About making the Academy Pontifical I shouldn't venture an opinion from this distance,' the Dominican cardinal demurred.

In his foreword to Giuseppe Alberigo's *A Brief History of Vatican II*, Jesuit historian John O'Malley said one undergraduate thought Vatican II was the pope's summer residence. Explaining the Second Vatican Council to those who did not witness the winds of John XXIII's prophecy is somewhat like teaching the fall of the Iron Curtain to students born after 1990. I visited Berlin in 1994 as an exchange student to see the remains of the Cold War division, and I knew Vatican II was an ecclesiastical council not a holiday castle, but I still needed a first-hand witness in plain-speaking English.

John Thornhill was waiting for me at the entrance to the retirement home for Marist priests in Hunters Hill, Montbel, where Woodbury first arrived as an eighteen-year-old to begin his studies for the priesthood. A Marist priest for sixty years and Woodbury's successor at the Aquinas Academy, John was the only person I have met who had sat at the table with Pope—now Saint —John Paul II.

'I've made some notes here for you,' John sifted through papers typed in large font once we were seated at his desk. 'See, this history reflects a whole big change taking place in Catholicism since the Second World War. Are you a Catholic?' he checked.

'I'm a new Catholic,' I answered. He wanted to know if I spoke the language. I did, but not fluently.

John's story began as a young Australian Marist in the overcrowded universities and student residences of Rome in the fifties. Postwar prosperity had opened the floodgate for seminarians around the world to study in Rome. John was twenty-four, awakening to the history of ideas and culture and forming an intellectual kinship with two of the early twentieth century's most influential English historians, Arnold Toynbee and Christopher Dawson.

'Toynbee had a two-volume abbreviated edition of his study of history. The British Council library was near our student house in Rome. I used to call in there and pick up a novel. They were very generous with their lendings. And I remember the first volume of Toynbee, how excited I was that someone was really talking about culture and civilisation, how they develop and how they go forward and backward. That led me to write my thesis about him.'

John wrote his doctoral dissertation on Toynbee's philosophy of history at the Angelicum where Woodbury had been a student. He attended lectures by Woodbury's old supervisor, Garrigou-Lagrange, but was persuaded by Toynbee that Thomism had to be placed in a continuum of historical and cultural change, as Saint Thomas himself had attempted to respond to the intellectual challenges of his day by reconciling Plato and Aristotle.

'Saint Thomas was involved in a great movement of change in his time,' John explained. 'But he disagreed with Aristotle in something very basic. For Aristotle, the basic thing to investigate in metaphysics is substance. But Saint Thomas says there's something more radical than that. It's the act of existence. Saint Thomas holds that there's a real distinction between what the thing is, its essence, and the actual existence that makes it big up there in the real.'

His eyesight and hearing were fading, but John was breathing life into big dead philosophers up there, making them real like spinach leaves on canvas, like Rilke saying the name of a jug.

'You can't have a concept of existence. You can only know it indirectly. I know that you exist,' he squinted. 'I know my books exist,' he looked over to his bookshelves opposite us. 'But what you *are*, isn't your existence. What you are is in God's mind forever. Before ever the world was made. What my books have in every page, every letter, is in God's mind. But that it *exists* is a radical thing.'

'What would Aristotle have said?' I sounded like the von Trapp children nagging their governess to keep saying nice things in a thunderstorm.

'Aristotle said—well, now how do I put it?' He cleared his throat. 'In things,' John started again, 'you've got to distinguish between what's potential and what's actual. Aristotle said that a blind man who's asleep hasn't got the potential to see. But a man who's not blind and is asleep has the potential to see. So there's a capacity in him that's activated when he's awake.'

'And he's got his eyes open,' I said thinking of the Matisse tour.

'So this is very basic to the whole Aristotelian thing,' John continued his summary of essence. 'And Saint Thomas takes a step forward and says existence is an act,' he clapped his hands together, 'that comes after essence not in time but in thought.'

'My understanding is that he moved away from Platonic philosophy and incorporated Aristotle at a time when not many medieval philosophers did, so he was radical in that sense,' I contributed.

'Most of his thought *was* shaped by Aristotle, but this final distinction between existence and essence was something Aristotle didn't make.'

'So what you were saying before about the books and me,' I went back to the nice things, 'the essence is what God sees, the existence is what you see?'

'The essence is already defined in God's mind,' John answered. 'It's a possible thing. The difference between a possible and an actual thing is the existence. Now if we knew existence we'd know God because God is existence without limit. The wonder of existence, as we're talking now, is that these books were in God's mind but now they're real.'

'Yeah,' I slowly dawned.

'But they're very tiny, little realisations of the act of existence. Yours is a very wonderful realisation of the act of existence. Very different.'

I got that. 'Every thing unique.'

'But this act of existence, which we see has degrees, in the end God is only existence. God is existence. Full stop.'

'So God doesn't have essence?'

'God's essence is existence.'

'And that's what Saint Thomas said?'

'That's what Saint Thomas said.'

'And Aristotle didn't talk about existence? He only talked about essence?' I double-checked.

'Aristotle didn't move that far.'

John defended his doctoral thesis in 1958, a week after his mother died in Australia. Unlike Woodbury, he didn't make it home in time to see her. He spent a year in a Melbourne parish ministering to migrants who had been in displaced persons' camps in Europe before he returned to Toongabbie to teach theology at the seminary where he had been a student. He used Woodbury's philosophical texts and caught the train to the city once a week to hear Woodbury lecture. He started publishing his ideas on Toynbee, integrating Saint Thomas with contemporary theology.

John's career spanning six decades included a stint on Rome's International Theological Commission by appointment of Pope John Paul II —a saint with human shortcomings, in John's first-hand eyes.

'And we need to know those,' he stressed. 'If the church acknowledged it made mistakes and didn't have the answer to all the questions, it would have far more respect than it has at present. Here's a mistake that should be trumpeted on high: in 1950 Pius XII put out an encyclical, *Humani Generis*, condemning the new theology, which was being promoted in France. The new theologians, Henri de Lubac and others, were going back to the early fathers and the rich traditions of the church. A lot of people now think Garrigou-Lagrange wrote the encyclical. I was a student when that was read in the dining room in Toongabbie.'

'What was the impact of that in the dining room?'

'Well, most of the Marists were pretty conservative and they were a bit frightened by this new theology. The Marist superior general at the time, an American and the first non-Frenchman, Alcime Cyr, panicked and sent all the French seminary professors to Senegal.'

'And what did you think when you were listening?'

'I didn't know. See, I hadn't got onto my historical approach. And Garrigou-Lagrange was Woodbury's great teacher, although I didn't know about him being the ghostwriter at that stage. I thought, *It can't all be bad.* That was my reaction.'

The 'new theology' condemned in 1950 at the hand of Woodbury's old teacher and rehabilitated at Vatican II was the topic of the 1965 inauguration of the Aquinas Academy. The American superior general of the Society of Mary, Joseph Buckley, who had attended the first three sessions of the council and was on his way to the final session, gave the opening address in front of his old friend from the Angelicum. Buckley told Woodbury's students that their teacher had converted him to Thomism as a student, thanking him for the many informative lectures he gave, 'walking frontwards and backwards, up and down the path or the walk beside our International House of Studies in Rome, and he carried a great big key, a key about so long,' Buckley was taking off the Doc, too, 'and he used to use that to gesture with.' Woodbury had asked Buckley to speak about the work of the council: 'There is a very strong trend in the Council against the Thomism that Father Woodbury, and I, love deeply and believe in very much.' Buckley described the many conciliar speeches calling for a new system of philosophy and theology without putting forward any new ideas, the impatient signals in St Peter's at the Dominican master general speaking in support of Saint Thomas. 'I think it is wonderful that there is someone like Father Woodbury,' he continued, who can assure 'a proper understanding of Saint Thomas, not only among the clergy, and the Sisters and Brothers, but among the laity, so that there is still a strong phalanx of true Thomists in the Church.' Buckley had a parting word for Woodbury. 'Whether or not you succeed in founding this wonderful school of theology and philosophy, even a university,' he hoped 'you are seeing into the future of something that will come from your efforts here in Sydney.'

Privately, however, Buckley raised concerns with Woodbury that his good work of teaching true Thomists was being undone by his monopoly on the Academy.

Woodbury confided in his confrère, Radford, who had taught for Woodbury at the Academy and with whom he had discussed plans for a second campus at Parramatta before Radford's appointment as rector at Toongabbie. Seventeen years younger than Woodbury,

Radford was placed in a delicate triangle. Woodbury asked that he write to Buckley and with Woodbury's consent he approached the provincial, Webber, who advised Radford to give an honest appraisal of the matter as he had observed in his relationship with Woodbury at the Academy. Radford took his time and when he did write, almost two months after Buckley's visit in a three-paged typed document, he chose his words carefully. Woodbury was a brilliant philosopher 'with an unerring penetration which would rarely be equalled in the world' coupled with his expository talents as a teacher. He was, in short, a genius with an enthusiasm for his subject that accounted for the success of the Aquinas Academy. His personality, Radford continued, was emotionally immature and this, combined with his gifts, attracted a small circle of loyal followers who completed his identity by becoming 'his intellectual satellites.' A larger fringe of students, less emotionally involved, Radford observed, 'are genuinely attracted by the doctrine and the quality of the teaching.' They came for a few years and then went off, grateful for what they had received, to integrate it into their lives. Woodbury's whole self was invested in Thomism such that he regarded critics of Thomism as both intellectual and personal opponents, creating a perception that the Academy was 'a citadel in perpetual siege.' Radford recommended to Buckley that the Aquinas Academy not become a pontifical institute due to its 'intensely personal character.' Woodbury was a man of great generosity and sincerity, he summed up, but at sixty-six he lacked the awareness to address the problems of the Academy's longevity. 'When he leaves the scene,' Radford concluded, the Academy 'will change its character or else go out of existence.'

Radford's description of 'a citadel in perpetual siege' begged Buckley's reply. The superior general and Thomist convert, in his address to Academy students, had called for a 'strong phalanx of true Thomists in the Church.' Military combat, like medical symptoms, was the language of a medieval church. Woodbury compared Andersonian philosophy to a malignant tumour, Bishop Muldoon thought the city had gone mad, Buckley praised the formation of Thomist foot soldiers and Radford diagnosed a siege mentality in Gloucester Street. The church needed not only a new Pentecost. It needed new tongues.

Woodbury's talk with his old friend and fellow Thomist might have led him, at sixty-six, to walk into the lecture hall one evening and lament, *I don't know. Maybe Saint Thomas can't solve the rat epidemic in Sydney, or the danger of apostasy in the church, or mend what fell off the wall and landed in a hundred pieces.* His deep compassion for his students and family might have shone its own light in Gloucester Street not through wit, but a heart that knew how to weep. He didn't need the approval of the pope or Saint Thomas, or anyone else including his gifted students carrying on his work at home and abroad. He needed a wise companion to hold his broken pieces that no glue could put back together again: a child's mispronounced word, a cow's indifferent gaze, Matisse's sensible scissors. Even the million and a half words of the *Summa theologiae* remained unfinished like straw, Saint Thomas said, after God wove a spell on him and he stayed silent.

Instead he fell headlong into an affair over an American nun, a bishop and an unfortunate letter. When Margaret Gorman, a Sister of the Society of the Sacred Heart and professor of psychology from Newton College in Massachusetts, visited Sydney for a lecture tour at the end of 1966 and spoke on national television about the inadequacy of language and symbols for God, one of Woodbury's students wrote to Bishop Muldoon. Gorman had published a book on contemporary Thomism, based on her doctoral thesis, but was apparently not a true Thomist. The bishop said she was mad, banning her 'near-heresies' from the archdiocese and condemning her, in the words of Saint Paul, to hell. Muldoon's reply was copied and circulated in Catholic mailboxes and editors' desks of the *Sun Herald*, *Sydney Morning Herald* and the *Catholic Weekly*, landing the bishop in a storm at a public meeting in support of Gorman. His qualified apology didn't go far enough for some who spilled their rage in ink to newspapers for months after.

Woodbury wrote to the editor of the *Sydney Morning Herald* to discredit the smears against the Academy, refuting any part by Academicians in the circulation of Muldoon's letter, but otherwise channelled his disgust into plans for pontifical accreditation. In June 1967 he sent the new provincial, John Glynn, an outline of his proposal and garnered letters of support from former students with their own academic credentials to speak for themselves. The benefit of such an accredited institute, Woodbury wrote to Glynn as he had written repeatedly to his superiors, would be that more religious would be inclined to attend. There were already Paulist and Capuchin students at the Academy. Why not Marist students from Toongabbie? 'Here they would rub shoulders with lay students, in many cases abler than themselves and I am perfectly certain that they would get a better Philosophy course here than anywhere else. Also the staff at Toongabbie could be proportionately reduced, thus saving manpower.' Woodbury quoted the Spanish Dominican master general, Aniceto Fernández, whose words on Saint Thomas were out of favour with some in the council. Fernández had visited the Academy in March 1967 and declared it 'the best thing of the intellectual order that I have seen during my visit to Australasia.' Woodbury estimated that student enrollments would jump to a thousand by 1970 if given pontifical status. Lay bequests from former Academicians would follow.

Glynn was more enthusiastic than Harcombe and Webber before him. He replied to each letter of support from alumni around Australia and abroad. John O'Dwyer, professor of physics at Southern Illinois University, told Glynn he had attended the Academy for ten years after returning from postgraduate studies in England in 1951. 'In my own field it is something of a necessity that scientists be brought to intellectual battle with the very weapons in which they themselves take great pride, and no man has yet accomplished this as has Saint Thomas Aquinas.' Alex Reichel, a senior lecturer in applied mathematics at University of Sydney, said Saint Thomas had helped him in his teaching and he expressed grave concern for the lives of Catholic students. 'To the extent that they think about the Church at all, many young people within this University appear to be bewildered by the cacophony of irreconcilable voices captured between the paper backs of countless books,' he wrote. 'Among many of them the "beatnik" spirit seems firmly entrenched.' Glynn agreed with Reichel. 'If this upgrading of the Academy was the only achievement of my term of office as Provincial, I believe I would be offering something of tremendous value to the people of Sydney and the Church in Australia.'

Timothy Suttor urged Glynn on from Toronto where he had taken up his appointment in theology two years earlier. He mentioned Gilroy's plans in 1947 to establish a Catholic university at Mona Vale under the Holy Cross Fathers while Suttor was teaching in the arts faculty at the University of Sydney. 'Do not say, Australia is a small country. Set an Institute in Sydney, and its country is the English language, the biggest country in the Church.' The scholarships set up by Melbourne's Archbishop Mannix for Catholic students to travel abroad had resulted in the kind of intellectual conformism that Reginald Batten described to Cardinal Browne, 'the looseness touching fundamentals and the self-importance in passing judgment on the Christian tradition, which mark the cult of modernity. I do not say for a moment,' Suttor finished, that a Catholic university 'will be enough in itself to stop the rot, but I do say you will never stop the rot without this.' Like rats gnawing at the pillars of society, intellectual rot—without Thomistic rigour—would continue to prevail in Sydney.

A swing to Thomistic music might also stop the rot of modern pop, predicted another student of the Academy, Pete Cruzado, a Filipino-born singer interviewed in the *Catholic Weekly* in November 1969. Whereas Thomistic philosophy had given 'order and dignity and proper expression' to Beethoven and other classical masters, most modern music was influenced by Kant and existentialism. Take the latest Beatles song, 'Octopus Garden,' for example, which was imaginative but devoid of reality. 'I'm not knocking the Beatles,' said Cruz. 'They show tremendous imagination, ingenuity and ability. But if they're looking for happiness they won't find it by running away from reality into an Octopus Garden or Yellow Submarine.' A movement back to the Thomistic philosophy reflected in songs like Rodgers and Hammerstein's 'You'll Never Walk Alone' was apparent in American composers Rod McKuen and Burt Bacharach, Cruz told the newspaper. 'You can feel a crying in McKuen's music. He's tending towards reality although it's not necessarily Thomistic-oriented.'

In May 1970 the *Australian Financial Review* interviewed Woodbury for a feature article on fringe-dwellers in modern secular Australian democracy. The four-part series by John Edwards was a survey of various 'eccentrics,' who occupied the political periphery of Australian society. Lined up alongside Woodbury and the Academy were the Henry George League, the Douglas Social Credit groups and the British Israel World Foundation, each bucking the general consensus that resulted in political apathy. 'Politicians may posture and strike histrionic poses,' Edwards wrote, 'but most people know that the Public Service is the ruling elite in Australia; that far from being a humble army of clerks it formulates policies, persuades Ministers to accept them, and then loyally administers them.' All four 'protesters' were chosen because of their apparent ideological paradoxes: 'adventist-imperialists, liberal social credit and anti-semitic social credit, Thomist Georgism; strange combinations which call into question our notions of the connectedness of elements in an ideology.' Woodbury was not only an outsider to Australian democracy; he was also an ideological misfit in the Australian church, 'as remote from the Irish obscurantism that typifies the conservatives as he is from the theological convulsions that have produced the liberals. Now in his late sixties he is white haired, lean and intense with the manner of an intellectual and a reformer.' 'If I walked down Martin Place,' the newspaper quoted Woodbury, 'and asked people if God exists, they would not say yes or no. They would say they were not sure.' It was this public nose wrinkling at Aquinas's proof of God's existence that drove his dissent towards modern universities and secular democracies. Wrinkled noses plus Thomistic certitude: 'It is not merely that I am right,' Woodbury summed up, 'it is that I cannot possibly be wrong.'

Woodbury made one last leap after another piece of his life fell away. His younger sister Cecily, with whom he had shared a long correspondence and infrequent visits, died in Port Moresby. In one of her last letters to Austin in August 1967, which she signed with her childhood nickname 'Scampie' instead of her religious name 'Leo,' she mentioned her opaque faith. 'The dear Lord still keeps me waiting, but please God one day it will be better.' She remembered family members and asked her brother at the end of her letter, 'Have you the proofs of the existence of God for me Austin?' Three years later, in March 1970, she wrote to congratulate him on the silver jubilee of the Academy. She had poured her prayers into his work, like her mother before her, but was lost in the dark after more than four decades as a missionary sister. She wrote of the weather, family and Austin's health and offered her prayers for him at daily mass, 'even though I am as dry as a bone. Goodbye now and God bless,' she ended, 'your loving Scampie.' She died in November that year. Austin found sympathy from family and friends, but he hadn't been able to show his little sister that God was really *there*.

Portrait of Austin Woodbury SM

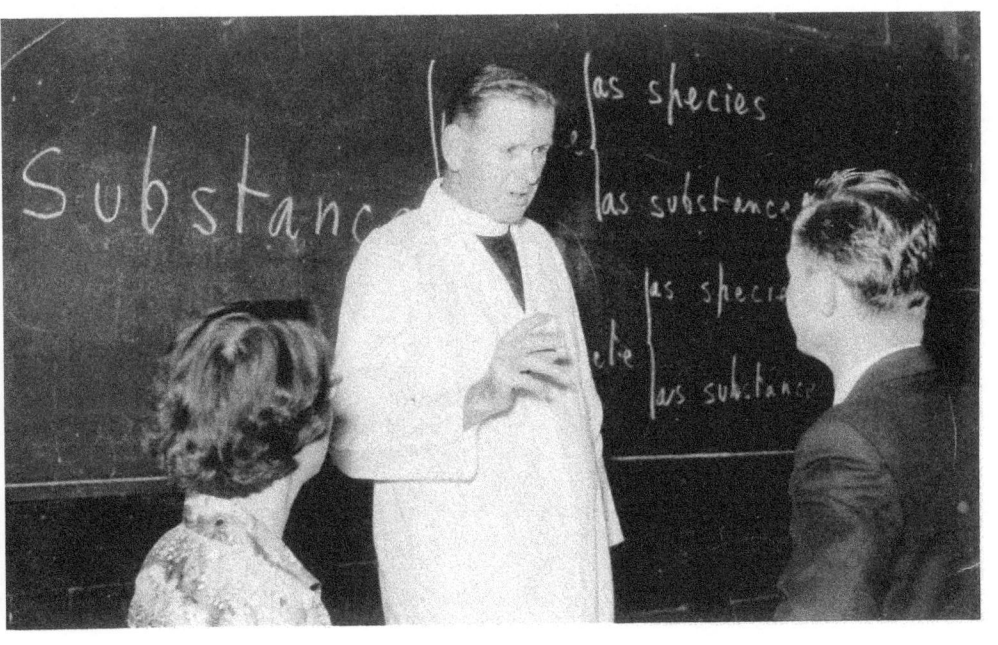

Austin Woodbury SM teaching

Patricia Woodbury OP with Michael Whelan SM

John Thornhill SM

Allan Connors SM

Kevin Bates SM

Michael Whelan SM

Marie Biddle RSJ welcoming Bishop Manning and guests to blessing of Mary MacKillop Hermitage

In the months after Cecily's death, Woodbury wrote—in English, Latin, Italian and French—to his provincial, to both the dean of philosophy and the rector of the Angelicum, and to the prefect of the Sacred Congregation of Seminaries and Universities. At seventy-two Woodbury was going back to Rome. His students had paid his fare so he only needed his provincial's permission to pursue the Academy's affiliation with his alma mater, which in the meantime had been granted its own pontifical title by the late Pope John XXIII. Known variously as a college since the sixteenth century and an institute in Woodbury's day, the Angelicum received its full Latin name of Pontifical University of Saint Thomas in the City a few months before the pope died, but the colloquial term stuck. When Woodbury arrived in Rome at the end of May 1971 for his meeting with Cardinal Garrone, the French prefect of the Sacred Congregation who had replaced Pizzardo, Garrone's secretary told Woodbury 'it is well recognised in the Sacred Congregation that the courses of Philosophy at the Aquinas Academy in Sydney are superior to those delivered at the University of Saint Thomas in Rome.' Woodbury reported his 'off the record' remark to the provincial along with a summary of the two meetings with Garrone, who had assured Woodbury of the Sacred Congregation's interest in an application for affiliation that the Angelicum would need to make on behalf of the Aquinas Academy. Garrone had also said, Woodbury quoted him, 'most of the contemporary philosophies would result in the destruction of the Church.'

Woodbury requested permission to travel to Rome again in 1974, paid for by his students, to attend the world congress of Thomistic philosophers in the seventh centenary of Saint Thomas's death. On arrival in Rome Woodbury was hospitalised with bronchitis and asthma and had to miss most of the congress. He wrote on 20 April from his hospital bed to the provincial, Peter Guiren, 'The Pope is attending it today: sorry to miss that.' The shaky handwriting resembled his mother's last letters and the sting at not being able to see the pope was a poignant end to his journey in Rome where he had first seen another pope, writing in red ink above the headline he sent back to his mother. Woodbury was readmitted to hospital at the beginning of June, delaying his departure home. When he returned to Sydney Guiren informed him that John Thornhill had been appointed principal of the Aquinas Academy. Woodbury's doctor, Guiren told him, had advised Guiren that Woodbury could not continue his responsibilities at the Academy. Guiren hoped 'God will spare you to be with us for many years to come.'

Woodbury was discharged from St Vincent's hospital to attend the 1975 inaugural mass and reception in his honour. Thornhill preached the sermon and acknowledged Woodbury's gifts in interpreting the insights of Saint Thomas. 'Aquinas was a revolutionary in his time, in introducing the Aristotelian spirit to Christian thought: a spirit which takes this world seriously – as opposed to the Platonic tendency not to take this world seriously in its concern to pursue eternal realities. Aquinas took the physical world seriously,' Thornhill said. 'He took natural wisdom seriously; and that seriousness made it possible for him to use the resources of that wisdom to make a contribution to theological science which led the Second Vatican Council to declare him the believer's greatest guide in the study of the mysteries of the faith.' Saint Thomas's system of knowing, which the council documents affirmed despite attempts to dismantle Thomism in the seminaries, 'avoided both extremes, that of an incomplete Platonism and that of a one-eyed secularism, and pointed the way to the true wisdom the world needed so much,' Thornhill finished on a note that became the hallmark of his own efforts to make Saint Thomas real in the present.

It was left to Thornhill to continue the negotiations for the Academy's affiliation with his and Woodbury's old university. During an overseas sabbatical in 1975 Thornhill met with delegates of the Angelicum and Sacred Congregation in Rome. Back in Sydney he wrote to Cardinal Freeman requesting that the matter of the affiliation be proposed to the Australian Catholic bishops' conference and seeking the *nihil obstat* from the Australian bishops. At the end of 1977 the deal was signed *ad experimentum* for four years and the first intake of students in the baccalaureate of philosophy enrolled in 1978.

Woodbury lived to see his dream fulfilled but not to see his first two students graduate. Terry Fitzgerald, who worked in the post office, attended lectures, handed out notes and made cups of tea for years at the Academy with a young family at home and involvement as a lay Dominican, graduated with his degree at the end of 1984. Of all the obituaries and tributes that flowed into the Australian province of the Society of Mary after Woodbury died at the age of seventy-nine, Terry Fitzgerald's stands out for its expression of a true vocation. 'I always instinctively felt that when many familiarly styled him "Doc," he wished to be regarded simply as *father* since that is what he was, a humble priest of God.'

'There is no doubt that the pursuit of wisdom was the overriding passion of Austin Woodbury's life,' John Thornhill said in his panegyric at St Patrick's next door to the Academy where Woodbury had lived for thirty years before his retirement to Hunters Hill. Thornhill quoted the Australian poet, James McAuley, who had told him that in a discussion with Woodbury of the nature of poetry he had found him 'the most enlightening man' McAuley had met. Woodbury was also a man, Thornhill said, 'subject like all of us, to human frailty.' He commended him to 'the living God, whose mystery filled Austin Woodbury with such awe,' and in whom 'his great mind and very human heart' could rest.

9
After Thomas

Bernard McGinn's biography of Thomas Aquinas's *Summa theologiae* catalogues fourteen strands of Thomism in chronological order: First Thomism, Byzantine Thomism, Jewish Thomism, Second Thomism, Chinese Thomism, Suarezian Thomism, Neothomism, Monumental Thomism, Twenty-Four-Thesis Thomism, Strict-Observance Thomism, Revived Thomism, Metaphysical Thomism, Transcendental Thomism and Analytical Thomism. To the uninitiated, Aquinas apparently instigated a Thomist reformation that spread with the printing press from west to east culminating in the nailing of the twenty-four theses to the papal door on the eve of a world war before splitting off, like nation states from empires, into twentieth-century borders. McGinn even cites a recent phenomenon of Taliban Thomism.

One of the myths in Woodbury's day, which McGinn puts to rest, is that the sixteenth-century Council of Trent ushered in the era of Neothomism. The story of the *Summa* being placed next to the gospel on the altar of St Peter's was manufactured by later popes and was simply not true, McGinn says. Dominicans, Franciscans and Augustinians were all represented at the council but later teaching orders, including Jesuits and Spanish Carmelites, popularised Saint Thomas in academic commentaries thanks to the modern invention of print. Comparisons with the Council of Trent were rife at the time of Vatican II amongst 'true Thomists'—or 'Strict-Observance Thomists' in McGinn's taxonomy—including the Marist superior general, Joseph Buckley, who repeated the myth of Saint Thomas on the altar at Trent in his inauguration speech at the Aquinas Academy.

Woodbury's niece, Rosemary Flannery, underwent her own Thomist reformation from Strict-Observance to Transcendentalism. As an eight-year-old, the youngest child of Austin's eldest brother, Herbert, Rosemary attended the opening of the Aquinas Academy with her parents in 1945. I imagined her swinging her restless shoes under the pews of St Patrick's waiting for the cardinal to finish so she could watch her tall uncle like she did when he came to say mass in the family church at Spencer. At seventeen she attended Academy classes in her first year of arts at Sydney, but something stole her attention away when she met Paul Flannery, a law student and president of the Newman Society who had also taken classes with Woodbury. They were introduced at a ball at Sancta Sophia college where the university chaplain and Woodbury's nemesis, Roger Pryke, hovered as chaperone. Pryke married them and baptised their first baby. Woodbury baptised their second. Two more children later, while teaching with the Jesuits at St Aloysius' college, Rosemary returned to the Aquinas Academy to enroll in the baccalaureate course affiliated with Woodbury's old university in Rome.

'I was brought up in the pre-Vatican II church where everything was black and white,' Rosemary explained to me. 'If Father said it was a blue sky or a black sky or a ginger sky you said, *Yes Father*. I think Uncle Austin wanted to broaden people's minds so that they could really think about their faith and understand what living the faith was.'

After taking Thomistic philosophy with her uncle's students who had become lay lecturers at the Academy, she went on to complete a theology degree studying the writings of Karl Rahner, Yves Congar and Edward Schillebeeckx, the 'new theologians' condemned by the pope in 1950 and rehabilitated at Vatican II.

'I was happy that I'd been a pre-Vatican II person, growing up in that very rigid black and white era, and coming into a grey orientation where the emphasis now is on being fully human rather than being fully Catholic. My children, who all attended Catholic schools, haven't got that background. They've got *God loves you*, which I agree with, but love is–' Rosemary's voice trailed off.

'What is love?' she asked the room.

I didn't know the answer.

'Love is a commitment to another person, other persons, to try and be there for one another in their search for God,' Rosemary said. 'As a child I felt very loved and very secure and very stable, but when I met Paul and the relationship we've had, I really felt personally loved and that is the love that I can then extrapolate to God, how God loves me, and how important it is to have that human love before you can fully understand the love of God.'

In between caring for her youngest daughter, Philippa, who sat next to me in her wheelchair joining our conversation, and caring for Paul up until he died a few months before I visited, Rosemary's favourite authors are all theologians, including the Swiss theologian, Hans Küng, whom Pope John Paul II banned from teaching Catholic theology. She also taught religion to boys at St Aloysius' college while she was principal of the junior school. 'Theology is my passion,' Rosemary expressed her motivation. 'It's helped me in my personal and teaching role. All your experience through life helps you see things differently or clearly.'

Women are the new theologians of the church, according to John Thornhill. 'We should be giving women far more roles so we get used to women exercising a guidance and leadership role,' John told me. 'If women are ordained, and I think it could be a very good thing, they'd have to have another liturgy altogether. Our liturgy is very much a masculine thing. A man stands up and tells people to sit down. That's not a woman's style. Women could be cardinals. Women could be on every commission of every diocese. Why doesn't the church do it?'

'Do you think it's fear?' I asked him.

'It's a power thing, security,' John said.

I quoted a sentence from the last chapter of his book, *Sign and Promise: A Theology of the Church for a Changing World*, about Mary and the church, something close to John's vocation as a Marist that took some time for him to come to treasure: 'From Mary the Church must learn the lesson of a courage that expresses itself in gentleness, availability and faithful witness.'

'There's courage in the *Magnificat*,' he responded after I had read his words to him. 'In Argentina, the generals prevailed on the church to stop saying the *Magnificat*. That's amazing, isn't it? And the bishops gave in. That's where Pope Francis is coming from. He went through all that.'

Devotion to Mary is not about the individual, John insisted. Mary is a model for the whole church, which has tended to follow Peter, the first pope. A Marian church has a different accent from a Petrine one.

'Mary is tenderness. The mercy of God. Such a solemn phrase. We hear it so many times. Francis says he'd like a revolution of tenderness. It's very telling. Tenderness is really mercy, but it's far more moving. Mercy is love in the presence of need.'

'Except you don't normally think of tenderness in a revolutionary sense,' I told him. 'You think of it as something domestic.'

'But he calls that a revolution,' John answered.

Afterwards I did my own *summa* of an Argentine pope and an Australian Marist and got a revolution of courage that bears witness to tenderness. Maybe that's also an equation of love.

Another graduate of the baccalaureate degree, Celestine Pooley, a Sister of Mercy for over sixty years, had just returned from a week retreat on medieval women mystics when I met her. Mechthild of Magdeburg, who wrote down her words about God in seven books, and Hadewijch of Antwerp, who named love in seven words, were beguines and contemporaries of Saint Thomas. Mechthild saw God as a 'flood' that begins, like the flow of women's bodies, in youth, diverts during gestation and ends in maturity. Similarly for Hadewijch, one of the names of love was a flowing river, which dries up and remains hidden in the 'unfaith' of those who no longer believe in the love of the beloved yet keep awake for love's sake. Saint Thomas's own experience of silence may have been induced by mystical excess or mental breakdown, or both as McGinn guesses, but while the beguines wrote in the vernacular rather than the scholastic style of First Thomists, their thirteenth-century words shared a God who wasn't there.

After Celestine's father left when she was two, she was raised by her mother and taught by Josephites to an intermediate level. Celestine was one of few girls who went on to finish her leaving certificate in the postwar years. She completed her secondary education with the Sisters of Mercy at St Patrick's alongside students in Sister Philomena's shorthand classes. Celestine studied music through high school and when she entered the Monte Sant' Angelo convent at sixteen, she was assigned to teach music. It was a ministry of obedience rather than choice, but Celestine chose to find enrichment in the relationships with her students in the absence of any real opportunities for intellectual or spiritual formation. More like 'malformation,' Celestine corrected me. 'Spiritual formation before Vatican II was rigid and not very inspiring.'

One intellectual pleasure of her music teaching was the thesis requirement for girls who elected to do music honours for the higher school certificate: talented and privileged students whose ideas and words Celestine guided to completion in preparation for their university studies.

After thirty years of teaching music Celestine saw her chance to change direction. Vatican II had turned the priest around to face the people, but it hadn't enabled Celestine to make the same use of opportunities for spiritual and professional development available to teachers at her school. She decided, in middle age, to make up for it on her own.

She knew of the Aquinas Academy from her school days at St Patrick's and some of the sisters who taught there had gone to Woodbury's lectures. Maybe if she had been assigned to St Patrick's instead of North Sydney she'd have gone sooner, but she wasted no time wondering about missed opportunities.

'I was teaching all day,' Celestine said. 'Music teachers start at eight and finish at five.'

'Plus marking at night!' I added.

'Yes, plus marking. But the Academy was more an interest to me. I went one night a week and did theology with John Thornhill. He was probably the biggest influence in my Academy days.'

A feature article in the *Catholic Weekly*, 'Nights at The Academy,' in May 1976 profiled the range of lay and religious students who joined Celestine in Thornhill's theology classes. Photographs showed John Thornhill chatting in the coffee break, pouring hot water into the cups of Lucy Cowhan, an accountant at the Mater hospital, an architect, Gerry Curran, and a secretary at St Vincent's hospital, Helen Scott. A working mother of adult children who travelled from Villawood each week to attend the theology class told the newspaper she had found 'great satisfaction' in reading the gospels. Richard Hallett, a naval architect and lay theologian, assisted Thornhill with the introductory course in theology. Peter Griffiths, a thirty-two-year-old father of three and metallurgist, was one of the newest students at the

Academy. There were doctors, nuns, university students, shopkeepers and school teachers taking units with Woodbury's old students. Anthony Keep, a bearded drummer in a Sydney band, music teacher and student of social welfare had signed up for philosophy as a newly married man. John Alchin was enrolled in ethics and ontology on top of his full-time load as a fourth-year medical student. And so the captions—and furrowed brows of concentration—went on.

When Celestine started to attend two nights a week John Thornhill suggested she was suited and ready to enroll in the newly affiliated baccalaureate programme in philosophy. 'I said, *You've got to be joking, philosophy?* That was seen to be up there,' Celestine explained. 'Well that meant a commitment of maybe three nights a week, but oh wow, when I think back to it, I just took to it like a duck to water. It was very narrow, absolutely Thomistic, but I probably couldn't have had a better background.'

Six years later Celestine joined the Academy's second crop of baccalaureate graduands. Her part time degree while teaching full time paid off *cum laude*. She had spent weekends and school holidays catching up on the reading in philosophy she had missed during term, taking public transport to the city after school and marking essays till late after her evening classes. Whether or not her students and fellow teachers celebrated her hard-earned distinction, Celestine had in hand her personal slip of a new beginning.

'It gave me my ticket to the next seventeen years of my life.' Celestine said. She moved out of the convent where she had lived with fifty others into a youth community she shared with a few other Mercy sisters. Then she decided to resign from teaching with nothing in view to step into. After thirty years she had to find a ministry to pay her way. John Thornhill was then teaching at the Catholic Theological Union in Hunters Hill where the Marist seminary at Toongabbie had transferred and secured Celestine a part-time job in the library. When Wilf Radford, who had taught for years in Gloucester Street, Toongabbie and finally Hunters Hill, became ill and needed someone to take his class, Celestine, freshly minted with thirty years of teaching under her belt, stepped into Radford's shoes to teach an introductory course in philosophy to seminarians.

As more lay people began to enroll in degrees, mothers with school-aged children were free to pursue their interest in theology.

Because many of them hadn't done any previous tertiary study, Celestine was recruited to teach a bridging course in basic study skills and logic. She also taught political philosophy comparing Marxism with Catholic social teaching. Then one of the lecturers suggested she enroll at Sydney University as a mature age masters student. She wrote her thesis on Aristotle while giving younger women at the Hunters Hill campus their first taste of higher education.

'From Aristotle you learn about the place of the senses. Even at this retreat,' Celestine referred to the week she had spent with Mechthild and Hadewijch, 'I told the retreat director that Aristotle first introduced some of these concepts and then Thomas Aquinas put the theology into it.'

The afternoon sun had shifted during our conversation and was glowing through the green glass of a Celtic cross on Celestine's windowsill.

'Philosophy taught me to read differently and more deeply,' Celestine summed up what she has been able to pass on to others. 'If someone asks me to write something, and I still do quite a bit of it, I don't do short.'

Her most recent piece was an article on Ebola orphans for *JustMercy*, an online publication of the Institute of Sisters of Mercy of Australia and Papua New Guinea. Celestine told me she does her research watching the news and finding newspaper articles, which she cuts out and keeps in folders usually stacked on the chair where I sat opposite her. The headline 'Do you want me?' in a story taken from the *New York Times* of a small girl, who had lost her parents and her sister to the Ebola virus and was photographed sitting alone on a bed in a children's home in Sierra Leone, jumped out at Celestine.

'When I saw that I just cried. Coming from the mouth of a little four-year-old.'

Celestine decided to write what she had seen.

'No child should ever have to utter these words!' she wrote in her article that mentioned the added risk for Ebola orphans of human trafficking. She quoted Saint Matthew's words attributed to Jesus, who touched children with his hands and said they should find safe homes. She also reflected on the words of Pope Francis who said that followers of Jesus had to learn how to weep.

Celestine's fellow Sisters of Mercy have a virtual prayer room on their website where intentions and petitions can be named with a candle, a star or a seed. After two careers in the classroom teaching music, Marx and Aristotle, Celestine now prays in her living room under a Celtic cross with all the named and unnamed hearts of those who have learnt how to weep.

'Is there something that has linked– because you've done so many different things, I mean from entering the convent at sixteen–'

'And do you know the amazing thing is, Julie,' Celestine answered my unfinished question with what I was really asking, 'most of them just happened to me. I have no regrets. For me, I say, *Be able to close a door and you're sure to*—I mean now that sounds naïve in this economic climate, and it probably is, but in my life I've closed one door sometimes not knowing if there's another door and there has been every time.'

She is not naïve about idealised vocations. 'They weren't the good old days,' Celestine said about the days before she discovered unheard of notes by Aquinas and the beguines, 'but it's not that I didn't learn something from it. It meant that for those thirty years that I did what I didn't want to do I could stick at it and find a lot of blessings in it. And then when opportunities opened up,' she said of her mid life decision to grasp what came, 'I was determined to educate myself in the way that I felt I wanted to beyond music.'

If I had to draw what I saw in the green glow of Celestine's living room, it would be her knuckled hands that marked teenage girls' words into the night while educating herself after school hours to teach philosophy to mothers and graduate with two university degrees and cut newspaper with scissors and tend virtual seeds with her tears. I would draw her hands of revolutionary courage.

10
Christian Growth

Teaching the faithful after Vatican II was not for the faint-hearted. In her three-volume study of American women religious, Sandra Schneiders lists some of the contenders that tried to replace Thomistic theology and philosophy, including 'process theology, Latin American liberation theology, feminism, a vastly expanded and deepened biblical culture, Eastern mystical approaches, and a host of psychological perspectives and techniques,' which contributed to authentic spiritual growth while masking a deeper spiritual crisis of fragmentation in the church.

The spiritual crisis affecting a system built on knowing rather than seeing needed new words—and a few new tools—but, above all, new courage in a disorienting time of unfaith. Schneiders, a Sister Servant of the Immaculate Heart, describes the passage of seven hundred years women religious like Celestine Pooley made in the years after Vatican II from the late middle ages of the beguines and the first Dominican women's communities founded by Saint Dominic in the early thirteenth century, to the belated opportunities for education alongside other Catholic adults in the last decades of the twentieth century. In the same generation that two Catholic university students met and married and raised their children to adulthood, whole communities of women experienced the death of what formerly they held to be a valid alternative to marriage and motherhood amid the postwar opportunities for women in the church. Though motivated by genuine spiritual idealism, Schneiders says, the aspiration for a higher education and professional role outside of domestic life led many young Catholic women to enter the convent. For these women more than any other canonically defined group in the church, the prophetic winds of change displaced traditions, cherished beliefs and identities in the space of a few decades. Yet among those who remained in religious life, Schneiders points to paradoxical signs of risk-taking and a relative absence of what she calls 'survival anxiety.'

Following her Carmelite contemporary, Constance FitzGerald, Schneiders attributes this apparent paradox of hope in the face of spiritual and vocational crisis to a mystical dark night in the tradition of Saint John of the Cross and those before him like the beguines, who learned to see in the hidden recesses of faith. FitzGerald's seminal article, 'Impasse and Dark Night,' published two decades after Vatican II, called for a spirituality anchored in stories of women, ageing, oppression, war in the false name of security, and the earth's wounds. A spirituality of impasse, like a revolution of courage, is not about the individual. It is for the whole church, for a whole world learning to see.

Two rainbow lorikeets kept pecking at the window of Allan Connors, a Marist priest, psychologist and former principal of the Aquinas Academy. I had interrupted their feeding time on the balcony when Allan was telling me about his first missionary assignment in Gundiwindi in the early fifties.

'That was in the days when you were supposed to threaten people with hell and death and all the rest of it. And I wasn't much good– there's one of my birds!'

The bonded pair only come looking for food after rain, Allan said. And only on weekdays.

He found something he was good at when the Marists opened a chapel and counselling room at Circular Quay in the years after Vatican II. He stripped the century-old walls back to their original sandstone, put the altar in the middle for the people to gather around and spent the next three years feeding weekday commuters and sending them back to their real lives instead of an imagined hell. It was his first taste of adult spirituality that inspired him to enroll in a psychology degree at the University of Sydney and later persuade the provincial, Peter Guiren, that he was better suited to the Aquinas Academy than the confessional.

Together with John Thornhill, Allan pioneered a Christian Growth Programme comprising weekly lectures in theology, psychology and spirituality that he expanded to suburban parishes all over Sydney and eventually regional centres throughout the eastern Australian states. Two decades after his failed mission in Gundiwindi, Allan found new words and a few new tools to reach people's experience of unfaith.

'You had women there whose babies had died at birth,' Allan explained one of his lecture topics on unbaptised infants who went to a place of limbo between heaven and hell, according to the catechism their mothers had memorised at school. 'And they had the idea, *I'll never see my baby again–*'

The sudden emotion in his voice after his exegesis of Saint Augustine's seven books on baptism caught me by surprise.

'Such relief, a real revelation to them,' Allan looked out the window behind me and I thought of the silent grief he'd helped lift for them and carried ever since.

He clocked up thousands of kilometers on his weekly circuits from Sydney to Wangaratta, Shepparton, Echuca and Bendigo blowing new winds into faithful communities of women and men who had real life questions that didn't have black and white answers. Completing another circuit from Narrabri to Inverell, Glen Innes and Tamworth as autumn trees shed their leaves, Allan wrote down what he saw: 'Cars arriving from Tenterfield'—'Guyra fog-bound'—'a flock of sheep wearing their little plastic coats' on the Moonbi range —'so vast a field, so little seed sown'—'will the big harvesters find a crop on the plains?' Not every question had an answer, but at least people were meeting, Catholics with their non-Catholic neighbours, in parish halls on weekday evenings to talk over a cup of tea about something other than the weather, their families and electoral issues.

The bishop of Wilcannia-Forbes had been worried about Catholic students in his diocese leaving for university, but who would teach them the faith when they grew up and left Sydney and the metropolitan networks behind them? 'In many areas of life country isolation is a big problem unrealised by many who are therefore not challenged by Vatican II in deep ways,' one woman wrote to Allan after he had visited her parish in Forbes. She had left Sydney as a young adult and, apart from her husband and one priest from a previous regional town where they had lived, she'd survived like Celestine Pooley for three decades without any intellectual or spiritual formation.

Allan's secretary, Leonie Waterson, attended the Christian Growth Programme as a mother of two primary school-aged sons. 'We knew a hint of something had happened with Vatican II, but the good news didn't seem to be blowing through our church at a parish level,' she told me.

Leonie had completed her secondary schooling at St Patrick's business college and became the first laywoman to be employed there, taking over the class that Mother Cleophas had taught during her time as principal. Leonie taught in the college for six years and then filled in as a relief teacher after her sons were born. Sister Philomena had long gone, so when Allan Connors needed a secretary at short notice it was the new principal of the business college, Sister Raphael, who arranged a replacement. Leonie went initially to help for a few weeks. She stayed on for the next two decades, fielding course enquiries, taking bookings and producing wax stencils of Allan's seven-page lecture notes before the dawn of electricity.

'The stencil had a cardboard backing sheet with patterned holes that would fit on the printing machine. Big, noisy, clunky thing, even then it belonged in a museum,' Leonie said. 'So there was the top wax sheet, then a sheet of black carbon so you could see what you were typing and it would also put an imprint onto the backing sheet that you could read to check. If you made a mistake you filled in the imprint with bright pink liquid wax and you had to keep it from attaching to the carbon underneath by running a pencil in behind, then blow *whooo-whooo-whooo*,' she puffed the air at her dining table, 'to get it dry. The liquid wax couldn't be gooey, but had to flow on evenly, so that you got the cleanest, corrected imprint possible.'

I sneezed. 'It sounds like an art project!'

'Yes, but because I'd been teaching and standards at St Patrick's were very high, I couldn't allow myself any more than two errors to a page. Mother Cleophas always insisted that if there were more than two corrections to a page the work needed to be redone. So from the wax stencil I would go out the back at the Harrington Street end of the building,' she went on, 'freezing in winter, no such thing as a heater, and on this great big old relic you would affix the holes on these little jutting out bits and be very careful to smooth it down carefully otherwise you'd get pleat marks across the copy. In the very early days you hand turned it and then at some point Allan lashed out and we got an electric one.'

Unlike Patricia Woodbury in the war, Leonie was able to run off all the lecture notes on the Academy's own Gestetner instead of going next door to the business college. It could well have been a hand-me-down from Sister Philomena. 'You inked it first,' Leonie continued, 'by turning the handle a couple of times and the ink would feed onto this printing cylinder and then the paper fed through as you turned the handle. You were out in this little cupboard of a room that had nothing else in it except reams and reams of coloured foolscap paper stacked high, a table to put the printed notes and if you stopped turning, it stopped printing!'

Despite workplace hazards of carbon, ink, wax and an unheated shoebox, Leonie had two more children while working at the Academy. If one of her young daughters was sick Leonie still went in to feed the Gestetner and made up a small bed outside the printing room. Later she was joined by a Sister of Mercy, Mary Crowe, then a single mother, Patricia Thompson, who stayed on as secretary through the nineties.

When Allan was appointed principal of the Aquinas Academy in 1981 he added summer schools to the expanding repertoire of adult education programmes. He asked permission from the new provincial, John Jago, to travel to England to attend Jesuit summer schools in theology, spirituality, scripture and psychology. Allan had lined up the English Catholic psychiatrist, Jack Dominian, to come to Sydney for the inaugural Aquinas Academy summer school in 1982. The visit to England would allow him to finalise arrangements for Dominian's visit as well as recruit other international guest speakers for future summer schools.

Jack Dominian's lecture tour in January 1982 attracted more spilled ink than the Gorman affair fifteen years earlier. The cardboard folder labelled 'Dominian visit' was the biggest in the Aquinas Academy's archive. Bulging with clipped articles and correspondence from the *Sydney Morning Herald* and the *Catholic Weekly* as well as a deluge of letters to the provincial, John Jago, the Dominian file exposed a fault line that had less to do with his subject of marriage than with the spiritual impasse facing post-conciliar Catholics.

'Are you aware of the fact that these notices (yellow and blue) are on display in abundance at St Patrick's?' one letter addressed the provincial. 'Do you know what kind of man Dr Jack Dominian is? Are you aware of his principles or rather total lack of them?' In case the provincial was uninformed, the letter enclosed white sheet extracts from Dominian's book, *Proposals for a New Sexual Ethic*, along with the yellow and blue notices found in the back of St Patrick's. 'What a blasphemous insult to have the Blessed Sacrament exposed in a Church where diabolical courses are advertised,' the letter finished.

The official spokesman for the archdiocese of Sydney, Father John Hill, said in the *Catholic Weekly* that Dominian was a competent psychiatrist and a committed Catholic and he publicly dissociated himself from denouncers of the Aquinas Academy sponsoring Dominian's visit. Alan Gill, the religious affairs reporter for the *Sydney Morning Herald*, said a thousand people had signed a petition to cancel the Dominian tour.

I stopped counting the letters in the end. So did Jago, who typed a generic reply to each correspondent restating Hill's points that Dominian's expertise fell in the area of his two lectures, 'Relationships and Spirituality' and 'Marriage, Faith and Love,' and that adults who chose to attend the lectures at St Joseph's college in Hunters Hill could expect to gain something from their attendance. For those wondering what it was all about, Marist Chapel sold fifty-cent reprints of Dominian's booklet, 'Growth in the Capacity to Love,' to commuters at Circular Quay.

When Pope Paul VI published his encyclical on the procreative purpose of married life, *Humanae vitae*, the Aquinas Academy sent a Latin letter of support to the pope on the feast day of Saint Thomas in the name of six lecturers and over four hundred students. The pope's secretary of state sent a Latin reply that Woodbury circulated in English translation to the signatories. Thirteen years later one of those signatories invited his son to hear Jack Dominian in Sydney. Terry Fitzgerald, who gave up his weekday evenings to help Woodbury, Thornhill and then Connors keep the Academy urn running while completing a degree in philosophy, introduced his son Tony, a high school teacher, to philosophy before taking him to the English psychiatrist's talks in the summer holidays.

'I remember Jack Dominion because he said something unforgettable in his talk,' Tony Fitzgerald told me. 'He said, *I have a fear of flying, and what I had to do about this was to see another psychiatrist.*'

After travelling twenty hours at high altitude, Dominian had to overcome placards and loud speakers at the protest rally on the grounds of St Joseph's where seven hundred adults had registered to attend his lectures.

'I never expected they'd turn up like that,' Allan said. 'But actually they did us a service because the more they protested the better we became known. I owe them a debt of gratitude really.'

He received notes of gratitude from women religious within and outside the Sydney archdiocese. Zelma Latta, a Sister of St Joseph of Orange, enclosed a card with a verse from the psalms and a copy of a letter she had written to the *Catholic Weekly* stating the insights into 'spirituality, interpersonal relationships, community and Christian marriage' she had gained from Dominian's lectures. Sister Philomena Mary, from the Convent of Mercy in Goulburn where Theresa Woodbury had died, said she'd been enriched by the experience of 'mingling in a super-Christian community' and listening to Dominian who 'made us all so much more sensitive to the great meaning of the Incarnation.' She hoped for 'many words of healing' to come after the Dominian storm.

The dean of philosophy at Saint Thomas's university in Rome noted his and the rector's surprise after reading Allan Connors's annual report for 1983 mentioning the lectures by Dominian, whose 'positions on some points in family morality seem not to be fully in conformity with the tradition of the Church. In this area,' the dean wrote, 'the responsibilities of Pontifical Faculties are, of course, particularly important.' Connors sent him the cassettes of Dominian's two talks at the 1982 summer school and referred him to Dominian's chapter in the pope's book. The dean replied after he had listened to the cassettes: 'I did not find myself entirely reassured by them.'

Edith Dominian accompanied her husband on his visit to Australia. A mother of four adult daughters, she brought a close presence to one of the Academy family, Pat Baker, who'd lost her mother at the age of four. In Pat's album of her Academy years my eye caught a group shot of her standing next to the Dominians with Allan Connors, Terry Fitzgerald and a Marist seminarian, John Gillen, behind them. Edith stood in the middle beside Jack with her right arm wrapped around Pat's waist. 'She was a real, lovely, motherly mother,' Pat said.

Pat also shared Jack's affection for cats. 'I remember in the middle of Jack's lecture in the hall at Hunters Hill when a cat walked down the middle aisle, he stopped and said to everyone so happily, *Oh look at the cat!*' She told me she kept in contact with the Dominians for many years after the summer school.

After Pat's mother died in 1945 she went to live with her Mauritian grandmother, who came to Australia as a refugee during the war in her seventies and spoke only French. She couldn't walk to mass, but she taught Pat her French prayers and how to welcome people of all faiths.

'In those days priests, ministers and rabbis used to visit the parish,' Pat explained. 'That was the done thing. So my grandmother used to give cups of tea or coffee to rabbis, to priests, to Jehovah's Witnesses, and I would translate for her because she couldn't speak English. And my grandmother used to say, *You must always be welcoming to these people because there is only one God and they pray to your God. So if you are rude to them you are being rude to God.*'

When Pat was fourteen and a half her grandmother died and she went to live with her aunt and uncle. She was on her own in the world and needed to support herself so the family sent her to St Patrick's business college to get typing skills. At sixteen she got her first adult job, like Patricia Woodbury, as a secretary in a doctor's office. She met her husband at eighteen and married a week off her nineteenth birthday. For the next sixteen years, Pat's husband forbade her going to mass. Her beloved cats were her only solace. Pat had married an alcoholic, she discovered, with a violent temper. His sudden death, when Pat was thirty-five, was a shock and a release at the same time. She went back to her old parish at St Patrick's after a sixteen-year absence to learn the mass all over again.

'It was almost like entering as a newcomer,' I pictured.

'It was. At school I was told if the host touches your teeth it's a mortal sin. And there were people chewing on it! I couldn't believe it.' Sister Raphael, who sent Leonie Waterson to work for Allan Connors, and Rosa Lopez, who sold pink-iced buns in the school canteen, invited Pat to the Christian Growth Programme at the Academy. 'I'd been away from my church family for all those years and there they were opening their arms to me and saying, *Come back*.'

Pat and her new family started going out for supper at Pancakes on the Rocks. Then one evening Pat suggested a social club and a show of hands went up. *Yes* to a football game at Hunters Hill with Allan Connors refereeing in white shorts and a whistle. *Yes* to a picnic at Bobbin Head with a row of pastel thermoses lining the tables. There were race days at Randwick, Zorba dancing at a Greek tavern, singalongs with seminarians around the piano, Easter retreats, Christmas masses and masses in honour of Saint Thomas Aquinas. They put on plays and handed out Thomas Aquinas awards with black and white copies of the painted saint glued onto wooden statues like an Academy Oscar. Pat got one for her volunteer work at the Academy, answering phone calls and taking money after hours and helping run summer schools with Allan and his travelling team on top of her full time office job.

'It was the soul of the place,' Pat said. Married and not married, nuns and seminarians, old and young. She remembered a tall, Indian woman in her nineties who attended the Christian Growth Programme and kept coming to courses until she died in her hundredth year. The spiritual and social hub filled the absences of Pat's earlier life. 'It's not until you lose something that you realise what you've lost. And if you're given the opportunity to get it back you appreciate it all the more. It's only then that you realise how much you missed it and how much your life felt barren without it.'

Pat still calls St Patrick's home almost forty years after returning to the fold. She has sung in the choir, read the scriptures, handed out communion and said the prayers in French for an international mass. Her grandmother's hospitality found a new table to serve.

'It's funny what life hands you,' Pat reflected. 'Sometimes you can make a difference yourself, but other times you can't. Certainly when you're small you can't. You really are in the lap of God.' Until one day a stray cat found her way down to the front all by herself and received a happy welcome in the middle of a lecture on love.

Christian growth had a ripple effect. From city parishes to country towns up and down the eastern states, faith formation traced imperceptible lines that surfaced years and sometimes decades after an initial immersion. One among countless others, Anne Bailey completed the Christian Growth Programme in Newcastle as a postulant with the Lochinvar Sisters of St Joseph nearly thirty years before graduating from San Francisco Theological Seminary with a masters degree in spiritual direction.

Sometimes the breeze blew in cross ripples. The Holy Name Catholic parish of Wahroonga, whose Dominican friars had taught at the Academy and posed in their habits for a commissioned portrait of Saint Thomas, offered the Christian Growth Programme twice through its Prouille parish primary school. Fifty people completed the course in 1983 and reported good things back to their Dominican parish priest. The parish council invited Connors and his team again the following year and sent brochures to parishioners through the primary school.

Mary and Patrick Kirkwood's children brought the brochure home from school. Mary went along to the day lectures and Patrick signed up for the evenings. Patrick had spent seven years studying philosophy and theology in the seminary of the Missionaries of the Sacred Heart before deciding not to go ahead with ordination. He met Mary Clements, a student at the Sydney Conservatorium, in the St Gregory Chorale. She asked him to the Mater hospital ball. He asked her to the Orson Welles film, *The Trial,* based on Franz Kafka's novel. Saint Gregory and Kafka were the perfect symbols for the movements in liturgical renewal and the psychological unravelling that followed in the wake of Vatican II.

'What happened at Vatican II had been in the pot boiling since probably the twenties,' Patrick told me. 'And I think it was psychologically very badly handled particularly the switch from Latin to English. It was almost a disaster for some people. And the other thing was that people had their devotions. They had the Benediction of the Blessed Sacrament, they had–'

'The Holy Name Society,' Mary said.

'Yes,' Patrick added, 'and they had all these societies and sodalities, and then almost overnight they all disappeared and all that psychological understructure that people's spiritual lives fed on.'

The decline in parish groups had already begun in the decade before Vatican II. At St Patrick's the Holy Name Society, a men's confraternity popular in many parishes, had ninety active members in 1943, seventy-four in 1952 and by 1961 had ceased to exist. The female equivalent, Sacred Heart Sodality, fared only slightly better from just over a hundred and twenty members in 1952 down to forty in 1961.

As sodalities disappeared the liturgical movement swelled. In 1970, heavily pregnant with their second child, Mary sang for Pope Paul VI at the papal mass at Randwick racecourse. Along with members of the St Gregory Chorale, she and Patrick had performed in two medieval liturgical dramas, the Play of Daniel and the Play of Herod, in the crypt of St Mary's cathedral with an ecumenical cast and crew of leading musical lights. Mary and Patrick had also joined the Singers of David, performing new liturgical music under the direction of Christian Brother Colin Smith and Gabrielle Healy, a Sister of the Good Samaritan.

'She was a real Chaucerian nun,' said Mary.

'Yes a medieval abbess,' Patrick agreed. 'She'd get Graeme Bell, the jazz musician, to come in and play with us.'

They travelled with the Singers to Queensland, staying with local families and performing in country halls like a medieval band of troubadors. Later they joined a parish home study group in the Paulian Association and Mary became part of a mothers' group led by a Good Samaritan sister, Anna Warlow, and a Loreto sister, Margaret Finlay. The Christian Growth Programme, for Mary and Patrick, rippled across their spiritual, liturgical and family lives.

Patrick lent me his course notes that Leonie Waterson had typed in wax. In the series on the beatitudes Patrick had written above the lecture on mercy: 'Allan Connors's favourite beatitude.'

Mercy, from the Hebrew *chesed*, Allan's lecture notes said, 'is the outgoing kindness of the heart of God.' The word occurs over a hundred and fifty times in the Hebrew scriptures and is connected most often with truth revealed not as intellectual knowledge, but 'complete fidelity to a promise, in the sense of being true to one's word,' a sentence Patrick had underlined in black ink.

'I think one of the wonderful things we've grown in ourselves,' Mary highlighted her own truth, 'is that, I feel, we are Christ to each other.'

Patrick has kept his deep interest in the Thomistic philosophy and theology he studied in the seminary, partly through his work on national broadcasting in religious programmes but also as a self-confessed 'freak' of the Transcendental Thomists following Canadian Jesuit Bernard Lonergan, who followed Aquinas.

'Every gem he finds he says, *I must tell you*,' Mary lowered her voice to a mock whisper while Patrick retrieved Lonergan from his bookshelf.

I took a piece of coconut slice Mary had made while Patrick described Lonergan's thoughts about the changes in human consciousness in history, science and philosophy since the medieval age.

'These changes have in general been resisted by churchmen for two reasons,' Patrick quoted Lonergan, circa 1972. 'The first reason commonly has been that churchmen had no real apprehension of the nature of these changes. The second reason has been that these changes commonly have been accompanied by a lack of intellectual conversion.'

'Chew that!' I bit into the coconut slice.

'This is where Lonergan jumped out of Jacques Maritain's circle,' Patrick continued, 'when Maritain was still in the Aquinas of the middle ages.'

'We found Thomas Aquinas, didn't we?' Mary jumped in.

'Yes, in Toulouse,' Patrick replied. 'We were there in the cathedral and I was wandering around and I looked at the front of the altar and there was a big glass screen and it said, *l'vrai corps de Saint Thomas d'Aquin*.'

'The whole body intact?' I asked.

'No!' Mary laughed.

'The sanctuary was roped off and there was this little man there with a broom and he had a little beret on and I said, *Excusez-moi*, is this the true body of Thomas Aquinas? *Oui, oui*,' Patrick switched to English with a French accent, '*Come, come*,' he gestured like the Frenchman in the beret. 'So he took us inside to the sanctuary, then he went to this door and opened it up and there was a room out the back, the size of a church, and it contained their reliquaries. And he opened up this drawer and there was a map of a skeleton and coloured in were all the bits of Saint Thomas they had so out there, under the altar, were all these bits.'

'So it really was the body?' I was stuck on the bits.

'Yes, it was the body of Saint Thomas Aquinas!'

'Well, all the coloured pieces of it,' I said.

Afterwards Mary brought me back up the front garden path to my car past a carved icon of a mother and infant set on a tree trunk. 'As the Spirit led you here, may the Spirit lead you from here,' she sent me off with outgoing words of kindness.

I took Patrick's lecture notes home and picked out some more gems. One on the beatitude of mourning defined the Greek word for comfort: 'It is the word which is used with the meaning to summon to one's side as a helper, a counsellor, a witness. It is the word meaning to invite to a banquet.' The 'work of grief,' Connors cited the phrase by Austrian Jewish psychiatrist Sigmund Freud, is being fed by one who knows how to weep and receiving 'the strength and beauty of God.'

But the tiniest gem wasn't written in wax and inked onto paper. It was when Allan said, 'I can't stand it,' stood up from his chair, walked to his kitchen and cut a thick slice of apple he held out for the bonded pair on the balcony in the round shape of a host.

11
New Faces

In a double-paged spread in the 'Family Magazine,' the *Catholic Weekly* announced a line-up of 'new faces for the Academy' for 1985. Along with the face of Saint Thomas Aquinas, painted in oil thirty years before by Barbara Hearn, and a side profile of the Swiss psychotherapist, CG Jung, there were also the faces of two Australian Marists fresh from postgraduate studies in the United States, Michael Whelan and Gerard Hall, and a Marist with two degrees from New Zealand, Tom Ryan. Whelan's course on 'Formative Spirituality,' the *Catholic Weekly* told readers of the 'Family Magazine,' would suit students who had completed the Christian Growth Programme and 'are trying to discover their identity more deeply, so that they can involve themselves in the life of the Church and society with greater fruitfulness and happiness.' Ryan's church history course was relevant to the changes taking place in the post-Vatican II era and would explore such questions as 'What kind of Church did Jesus found? What sort of Church, and in fact, churches, existed for the early Christians?' Hall was recruited to teach into the Christian Growth Programme in Strathfield and Drummoyne following its success in the Wahroonga parish the previous year.

Since the inaugural summer school with Jack Dominian, the annual event continued to attract distinguished international speakers on an expanding circuit. Gerard Egan, a priest and professor of psychology at Loyola University in Chicago, followed on Dominian's heels in 1983 to give a series of lectures in interpersonal communication and organisational psychology in Melbourne, Canberra, Brisbane and Wellington. Melbourne's diocesan newspaper, *The Advocate*, reported that seven hundred and fifty Catholics attended the summer school at

Sacré Coeur college to hear Egan speak on styles of communication in marriage that emphasised mutuality rather than political tactics of taking positions and personalising issues. 'Politics deals with the imposition of ideology, vying for scarce resources and generally controlling what goes on in other people's lives,' the Melbourne newspaper quoted Egan above a headline on the same page about the pope's address in Rome on human rights in his communist country and the sacrament of marriage as 'a reciprocal gift' between a couple.

Egan returned to Australia in 1984 to give counselling workshops in Sydney, Melbourne and Brisbane. In conjunction with Egan's second visit the Aquinas Academy offered a year's training programme in parish ministry including basic counselling and pastoral approaches to marriage anullments. Among the women religious who attended Allan Connors's role-plays with actors was Patricia Woodbury, who had started her adult education at the Academy almost forty years earlier.

Egan's visits to Australia didn't stir the same pot as Dominian's, but the aftertaste from the English psychiatrist's talks still lingered in some dioceses. When word leaked that the Aquinas Academy had invited husband and wife, James and Evelyn Whitehead, to teach in the 1985 summer schools on adult spiritual development, the archbishops of Sydney and Melbourne sought assurance from the Marist provincial, John Jago, that the Whiteheads' visit wasn't against ecclesiastical policy of ex-priests speaking on the public circuit. 'The Whiteheads are leading authorities on continuing education for ministry and are consultants to the Centre for Pastoral and Social Ministry at the University of Notre Dame. James Whitehead conducts programmes in the Institute of Pastoral Studies at Loyola University, Chicago,' Jago informed Archbishops Clancy and Little. James Whitehead was a former Jesuit scholastic, but hadn't been ordained according to the Jesuit professor of scripture at Loyola University, Father Thompson, whom Jago consulted. The Whiteheads also had ecumenical experience as facilitators and consultants to Episcopal groups 'and are in good standing with the official Church,' Jago said. 'I am most grateful for the information that you sent me,' Clancy wrote back. 'It has been most helpful.' Little was greatly relieved, too. 'Earlier this year I had been approached by another body to approve the proposed visit to Melbourne of Doctors James and Evelyn Whitehead. Inquiry at that time led me to conclude that Doctor James Whitehead served some time in priestly ministry. After much thought and discussion I have established a policy whereby this particular Church does not sponsor those who are generally described as "ex-priests,"' he told Jago. The authority of Father Thompson that James Whitehead had never been ordained a priest was assurance enough for Melbourne's archbishop.

The backlash against Jack Dominian's visit to Australia in 1982 didn't deter the Aquinas Academy from inviting Dominian back four years later. Pink leaflets at the back of Marist Chapel and St Patrick's advertised Dominian's lecture, 'The Capacity to Love,' and listed his credentials from Oxford, Cambridge, Lancaster and London and his many public lectures to the British Medical Association, World Health Organisation and the Wives of Members of the British Parliament. 'The supreme art of love is to ensure the constant freedom of those we serve,' said the pink leaflet. 'This is how God loves us and this is how we have to love others.' A red leaflet advertising Dominian's second lecture on 'The Human Personality of Christ' described Jesus as a man who dreamt in his sleep, coped with temptation, overcame his own ignorance and sometimes had difficult relationships with the people around him. The present pope, the red leaflet said, had invited Dominian to contribute a chapter in a book, *Fruitful and Responsible Love*, published under Wojtyla's name.

Dominian's scheduled visit provoked more pot-stirring. 'The main objection by critics is not about sexual matters,' Alan Gill wrote in the *Sydney Morning Herald* a fortnight ahead of Dominian's arrival. This time it was the title of Dominian's talk, 'The Human Personality of Christ,' that drew the ire of members of the Newman Graduates' Association who accused Dominian of near-heresy. 'The classic Christian view is that God became man,' said the association's president, Patrick Newman. 'What is creeping into the Church now is that a man became God.' The problem was interdisciplinary according to another committee member, Peter Birrell, a senior lecturer in psychology at the University of New South Wales. Dominian's clinical experience as a psychiatrist didn't qualify him to speak in academic areas of psychology. 'It's like bringing out an expert on garden worms and their biology to talk about gallbladder surgery,' Birrell explained. Allan Connors replied on record that Dominian's 'tremendous' competencies could be judged by the London hospital foundation for family life he ran with his eleven academic degrees.

The parish priest from St Benedict's, Broadway, Terence Purcell, took his campaign to stop Dominian coming to Sydney again all the way to the prefect of the Congregation of the Doctrine of the Faith, Cardinal Joseph Ratzinger, in Rome. 'The Aquinas Academy, Sydney, is conducted by the Marist Fathers,' Purcell informed Ratzinger in English and Latin at the end of 1985. He enclosed a copy of the Aquinas Academy flier advertising Dominian's lecture on 'The Human Personality of Christ' and highlighted in yellow the offending sentence: 'As a person Jesus felt the necessity of fulfilling the great human needs of loving and being loved, and feeling worthwhile to himself and others.' The theological problem, he wrote to Ratzinger, was whether Christ had a divine or a human personality. Christ was not a human person, Purcell said. He only had a human nature. When Purcell raised the matter with Archbishop Clancy in Sydney, Clancy told him there was nothing wrong with saying Christ had a human personality for the purposes of everyday speech. But, continued Purcell to Ratzinger, lecturers needed to use precise language to describe the hypostatic union. He included a photocopied page from the *Oxford English Dictionary* for the German cardinal, highlighting in yellow the words 'person, persona, personal, personality, personalise and personally.' Ratzinger might also have noticed the word 'persist' immediately preceding the yellow ones and which the *Oxford English Dictionary* defined as 'to continue firmly or obstinately (in opinion, course, doing) especially against remonstrance.'

In the end Dominian didn't make it onto the plane most probably not because of Purcell, but because he was still scared stiff of flying. Instead the main news items in the *Catholic Weekly* for the dates of Dominian's visit were the Polish pope's message of peace for 1986, the upcoming papal tour to Australia and the requiem mass for Bishop Muldoon at St Mary's cathedral. Still the publicity from the summer schools paid off in dividends for the Aquinas Academy. The *Catholic Weekly* reported over two thousand expected enrollments in Academy courses for 1986. The parishes of Pymble and Narrabeen were hosting the Christian Growth Programme for the first time and a thousand people were estimated to attend weekend seminars on Jung and the Myers-Briggs Personality Type Indicator.

The Academy's new faces from home and abroad delivered up-to-date expertise in theology, spirituality, history, sociology, psychology and pastoral ministry that complemented the credentials of lay lecturers teaching Thomistic philosophy to mostly mature age students like Terry Fitzgerald and Celestine Pooley. Woodbury's old university had granted 'definitive affiliation' with the Academy's baccalaureate in philosophy following an initial four-year trial, but dwindling enrollments prompted the provincial administration to rationalise and centralise its philosophy courses at the Catholic Theological Union. Marists could no longer justify the cost of running two separate philosophy degrees in the city and Hunters Hill with two sets of lecturers. In effect this meant that the Sydney College of Divinity empowered by the Australian higher education board, and not Saint Thomas's university empowered by the pope, would become the accrediting body for bachelor courses at the Aquinas Academy. Rather than terminate the affiliation with Rome, Connors told the incoming provincial, Garry Reynolds, it was let lapse according to Roman custom.

The decision to discontinue the Thomistic philosophy courses and affiliation was a painful and personal blow for Woodbury's students who had undertaken postgraduate studies overseas at their own financial and professional expense. The issue was not about degrees, Don Boland wrote to the provincial on behalf of fellow lecturers Alice Nelson, John Ziegler and Geoff Deegan, but the pursuit of wisdom. Not everyone who studied philosophy did so because they wanted vocational training. 'This is no doubt a very hard idea to get across in contemporary secular Australian society, where philosophy is rather taken to mean a consideration of vague theories and idle speculations, of no use much to anyone.' Why shift what wasn't broken? There would always be need for smaller numbers of contemplatives in the church's midst: men and women who desire 'first and foremost to know truth for its own sake, without thought about how he or she may put it to some use or good work.'

Raising up contemplatives, as poet James McAuley said, was the unseen work of prayer 'like radium in the dark.' Rationalising degree programmes in an increasingly secular higher education system was the work of administrative common sense. 'Yet somehow, between prayer and common sense / hearts may be touched, and lives have influence.'

Somewhere between prayer and common sense contemplatives came through the door of the Aquinas Academy. At fourteen, Aloysius Rego came to Australia with his family from Burma seeking freedom of religious education. While Woodbury was defending his reputation in the wake of the Gorman affair and petitioning the provincial for pontifical accreditation with the approval of the Spanish Dominican master general in town, Aloysius was waiting with his family for the Burmese government to approve their right to leave the country. When the military assassinated Burma's first president and his entire cabinet, foreign workers including missionaries had to leave. Catholic schools that Aloysius attended were nationalised overnight and Burmese replaced English as the language of instruction. Freedom of religion was tolerated, which meant that families could still go to church but school children had to clean hospitals and streets on Sundays. Aloysius's father worked for the only foreign enterprise that was permitted to stay, Pan American Airlines, but chose to uproot his family with the faith of a patriarch. He brought his wife and four children, two hundred British pounds and a hole in his ring that had held a Burmese ruby he'd had to give back to his country. The family arrived in Australia stateless, but with the help of his Pan American boss and a chance encounter with a fellow Burmese refugee at mass, Aloysius's father found work and a place to stay within a miraculous October weekend. The children could go back to Catholic schools. Someone was looking after Aloysius.

At twenty-five, Aloysius came to the Aquinas Academy seeking answers to big questions. Like Jack Soulsby from Cornwall, who had arrived in Australia at seventeen, Aloysius was making a life for himself as an engineer but felt something was missing. His brother had joined the Passionist order of his family's Marrickville parish and he had a cousin studying to be a Marist priest at the Hunters Hill seminary. A Passionist priest, a friend of Aloysius, was conducting a retreat for Marist students at Kincumber and invited Aloysius to come along. On his way to speak to the retreatants, the retreat director slipped a photocopied page from Thomas Merton's *Zen and the Birds of Appetite* under his door. Deeply affected by Merton's reflections, on his return home Aloysius found two more Merton books back in the Marrickville library, *The Silent Life* and Merton's autobiography, *The Seven Storey Mountain*. Later he found a stack more in the Pauline bookshop in the city where he worked for an engineering firm.

'There was some thought in the back of my head that I would like to be a person like Thomas Merton,' Aloysius told me when I visited him at the Carmelite retreat centre in the woods of Varroville. He even visited a Cistercian monastery wondering if he was cut out for a Trappist life in the woods like Merton.

He had heard of the philosophy classes at the Aquinas Academy and decided to start his search there. He enrolled two nights a week in an introduction to philosophy unit taught by Academy stalwart, Wilf Radford, in his mid sixties. The other students in the class were at least twenty years older than Aloysius. There were people closer to Aloysius's age in the spirituality courses, and in greater numbers than the handful studying philosophy, but he wanted nothing to do with them.

'The church wasn't answering my search. I thought philosophy was the answer. But I was more impressed by Father Wilf than by the course. I remember sitting there and thinking if philosophy can do that for Father Wilfred than that's what I want.'

He took other classes with Don Boland, John Ziegler, Geoff Deegan and Alice Nelson, using Woodbury's old notes and passing all the essays and exams without enrolling in the baccalaureate programme. He was after answers not a degree.

'There was this vague possibility I might be interested in religious life, but in the contemplative life because of the Merton influence,' Aloysius took off his glasses and put them down on the table where we were sitting in the retreat centre's upstairs lecture room.

One evening during the coffee break two Carmelite friars from Varroville turned up in their brown habits to advertise a two-week course on Saint Teresa of Ávila for the four hundredth anniversary of her death. Because of his shyness, Aloysius was standing in a corner avoiding all the people from the spirituality courses when one of the friars spotted him.

'I was sipping away my coffee, minding my own business, wanting nothing to do with friars or church or spirituality. One of the friars, John Venard Smith, approached me and invited me to come along to the series of lectures. I didn't know Saint Teresa existed, but I couldn't say no to the friar's invitation because I was always brought up to oblige an invitation or request especially when it was from priests and religious. I was drinking and shaking and because I couldn't say no I said, *Y-y-y-y-yes, Father.*'

Aloysius caught the train back to Marrickville furious with himself that he couldn't say no. Because he had said yes he showed up a few weeks later for the course with his heart raging against his body for not saying no.

'And from the opening sentences I fell in love with Teresa. Everything she was on about I wanted to say, *Yes, that's what I want. That's my search, too.*'

An Irish Carmelite, Eugene McCaffrey, and John Venard Smith from New Zealand taught the course on Saint Teresa. Secular order members attended the lectures alongside participants from the Christian Growth Programme and spirituality courses at the Academy. It was all over after two weeks in the mid winter of 1982, but Aloysius had fallen in love and knew he had to keep searching for what Teresa had. He kept working in the city and going to philosophy classes during the week, but on weekends a friend drove him to Varroville secretly so his family wouldn't find out.

'Going out in secret, that's Saint John of the Cross!' I laughed.

'There were none of those signs of habitation that you can see now. It was so rural. There were not many streetlights. It was pitch black at night. There was a dirt road–'

'It was like the end of the world,' I imagined.

'That's exactly how it was. The friars gave me a room in the old retreat centre, not the new refurbished one, and then they all disappeared. I remember it was so quiet. There were only cows. We had our own cattle back then. So quiet, but the noise was deafening. And it was coming out from inside.'

Aloysius saw Eugene during the day for spiritual direction, but the questions were an invitation, *Can you live this life? Is this for you? Come and see.*

'I loved the kind of life, but I also loved my work. So there was this tug between my work and my life and this life, but in a way there was no contest. I knew that all of that didn't give me the contentment I was seeking.'

Within six months of falling in love with Teresa, Aloysius entered the Carmelites as a postulant. At the end of his year of postulancy, one of the friars suggested he go back to his mother's home in Goa, India, in order to meet his mother's family before beginning his novitiate. Aloysius's father had met his Portuguese mother in Goa during a pilgrimage to venerate the relic of Saint Francis Xavier in 1952. Thirty-one years later, Aloysius visited the country of his mother's birth before making his vow of poverty.

'That was the dark night of my life going to India. From the time I landed in the country I was so shocked by the poverty, the squalor. If I could I would have got on the next plane and come straight back. I didn't know what I was dropped into.'

In Burma Aloysius had grown up in middle class comfort with servants in a third world country of twenty million people. But it was the poverty in a country of one billion people that broke him. When his father's cousin, a nun in Calcutta, invited him to visit both his body and his heart said no.

'I thought if I went I was so afraid my mind would snap. I thought I'd never re-emerge. I was living on the edge just waiting for the six weeks to finish so I could get right back here. It had a terrible, terrible effect on my psyche. I saw life in the raw when we take away all the tarting up of our lives. You see what's beyond that.'

When Aloysius came back to Marrickville he could barely tell his mentor, a Passionist priest, what he had seen.

'It's only until recently that I couldn't talk about this. I would choke. And I remember him saying to me, *Al why don't you go and join there?* And I told him I couldn't stand up in the pulpit and tell these people, *God loves you.* That would be blasphemy. I didn't know what kind of God that is.'

Aloysius took what he couldn't say to study theology in Melbourne. He was ordained five years later and spent a few years in retreat work at Varroville before the unspeakable drew him back to Melbourne with a deeper question about suffering. After studying Saint Thomas at the Aquinas Academy he wrote his doctoral thesis on another Dominican theologian, Edward Schillebeeckx, whose work had been banned from seminaries in 1950.

'Schillebeeckx was at the very early stages of a liberation theology. I would consider him one of the very early pioneers of liberation theology. When I read him he's very much into structural concerns with regard to poverty.'

'Did you answer the question?' I asked Aloysius.

'No, I haven't answered the question, but I've learnt how to live with the mystery better than I was able to,' he replied. 'My studies gave me a whole context in which to understand it better and live better with this reality, this dark mystery.'

While Aloysius was finishing his doctorate and teaching theology, the Polish pope declared the nineteenth-century Carmelite nun, Saint Thérèse of Lisieux, a doctor of the church joining the ranks of the church's two other women doctors: Saint Teresa of Ávila and the thirteenth-century Dominican Saint Catherine of Siena. Aloysius had first discovered Thérèse as a seminarian in his late twenties. After his doctorate he wrote a book on her spirituality.

'I found the simplicity of Thérèse very attractive. She's a twenty-four-year-old woman without any formal theological training writing about her life with God. Even now when I read Thérèse, I can't put her down. She speaks immediately to my heart. Thérèse is a friend I walk with all the time. When I'm afraid, when I'm going to do things I'm anxious about, I say, *Thérèse come with me*. I always have that sense she looks after me. She's my sister. Gives me that companionship that I need.'

'And John of the Cross and the others, are they less or more–'

'John I appreciate more intellectually. And Schillebeeckx fills my head, but it's Thérèse who has filled my heart and kept me on this journey.'

It was almost by accident, Aloysius said, that he found a new home at fourteen and later found Thomas Merton and Thomas Aquinas and Teresa and finally, Thérèse, the friend of his heart.

12
Mary's Song

St Patrick's, Church Hill, had been a spiritual home for three generations of Academy students. From the annual inauguration addresses of cardinals, bishops, apostolic delegates and superior generals on the feast day of Saint Thomas, to the weekday five-thirty masses before evening classes, to Woodbury's packed funeral that ground traffic to a halt in The Rocks, St Patrick's was a site of sacred memory and celebration.

Tom Ryan, parish priest of St Patrick's and one of the new faces at the Academy, gave the homily at the 1984 graduation mass for the affiliated degree in philosophy. There were two graduates in the baccalaureate that year, Terry Fitzgerald and Karl Callinan. The last six were due to finish the following year before the programme was shut down indefinitely. Another nine students received diplomas for the course in parish ministry that Patricia Woodbury completed the same year. The largest cohort was a class of a hundred and thirty school teachers who were awarded diplomas for a new catechetics course offered through the Academy and the Catholic education office. In his homily from the gospel of Saint John on the work of the Holy Spirit, Ryan didn't distinguish between vocational and intellectual pursuits. Instead he spoke about a creative tension in the gospel. 'Not one of you is asking where I am going,' Saint John quoted Jesus speaking to his followers on the eve of his death. 'But when the spirit of truth comes, she will guide you into all truth.'

'Right from the early Christian communities,' Ryan began, 'there is a tension between two forces: stability and development, the urge on the one hand to stop in the security of the truth, the opposite urge to break new boundaries in our understanding.' Sometimes it was the church that put the reins on new developments, Ryan was speaking a fortnight before Archbishop Little's letter banning 'ex-priests' from the archdiocese. 'Sometimes the Church is like Peter – being led by the Spirit where we would rather not go.' Both these urges were necessary or the church would die. Like Woodbury before them, he continued, Thornhill and Connors were 'following in the footsteps of Thomas Aquinas himself who enriched the faith by drawing on the riches of Greek and Arab philosophers in the middle ages.' Aquinas's own teaching was banned after his death by the archbishop of Paris, Ryan added. The work of the Aquinas Academy was a work of faith that depended on all it served, Ryan addressed the students of philosophy, theology, psychology, spirituality, history and education in the pews of St Patrick's. 'It depends on your urge to understand more the mystery of God incarnate working in our world,' he finished with words of revolutionary courage. 'We should never fear where the Spirit of God leads us because Christ walks at our side.'

A decade later at the fiftieth anniversary mass for the Aquinas Academy, it was the new principal, Kevin Bates, who delivered the homily. John Thornhill read the gospel message on the Good Samaritan summed up in a single line in the mass programme as 'the challenge to move from law to love.' Patricia Woodbury read the first reading from Saint Paul to the Philippians. The programme listed the communion hymn by Saint Thomas Aquinas, *Adoro Te Devote* ('Godhead here in Hiding'), translated by Gerard Manley Hopkins.

I imagined the procession of students from the Woodbury, Thornhill and Connors eras approaching the hidden reredos behind the main altar. It had been installed and blessed during the war, a few months before the Academy opened, but later had been covered over like Sleeping Beauty awaiting its final restoration. Jack Soulsby, who served as acolyte to Bishop Muldoon at the 1962 inauguration mass and was ordained at the altar seven years later, and Johno Johnson, former president of the Legislative Council, both paying their respects to their old teacher. Celestine Pooley, who waited three and half decades after her high school graduation at St Patrick's to graduate with her first university degree in the same church. Along with Patricia Woodbury no longer clothed in her habit, wearing a pink blouse pinned with her black and white Dominican cross, reading in her small sure voice the words of Saint Paul: 'You must shine out among people as stars lighting up the sky.' To shine by losing your life, Saint Paul said, 'pouring it out like a liquid offering to God.' And as the gifts of wine and bread were carried up to the altar by a married couple who had grown to be Christ to each other, the Marist priest and song writer who had stepped into big shoes as the new principal of the Academy sang the final verse of his own *Magnificat*: 'The promises God made long ago, capture the passion in our soul / The Word that God has spoken now takes flesh before our eyes / New love ignites the promises of old.'

Kevin Bates brought his gift of music to the Academy's work of adult education. He played the organ for Woodbury's funeral at St Patrick's after completing a masters degree at the Jesuit School of Theology in Berkeley.

'Very Marist,' Kevin said when I visited him at the Hunters Hill presbytery on the grounds where the first Marists are buried overlooking Tarban Creek. 'What do you want me to do?' he'd asked the provincial, Peter Guiren. 'Oh probably something about sacraments. Go and find something,' he'd been told.

After doing some research Kevin found a masters programme where he could study his love of the liturgy alongside liberation theology, jazz, folk, Black, Latin and indigenous music while learning to improvise in four chords during communion. He was a classically trained pianist from Geelong studying in Berkeley during the fall of Saigon. He grew his hair and rode a pushbike around campus.

When he returned to Australia, after some years working as the assistant novice master he helped develop the old Toongabbie seminary into a Marist retreat centre. Later he became Allan Connors's driver on the Canberra to Batemans Bay leg of the Christian Growth Programme. Like Con Woodbury driving his ageing uncle up and down convict roads, Kevin took the wheel while they discussed the needs of the church and the Academy. Perhaps they argued over the radio station, but they agreed that Kevin should take over as principal. He had already started playing his music in Allan's spirituality lectures and rebadging the summer schools as 'Happenings.' The *Catholic Weekly* advertised the 'happening' at Hunters Hill in 1991 with the Whiteheads back for two lectures on 'The Spirituality of the Negative Emotions' and 'The Spirituality of Sexuality.' There was a poetry seminar with the Marist priest and poet Noel Rowe, a poetry competition with a staggering thousand dollars for the best original religious poem, daily liturgy and music by Kevin Bates and use of the St Joseph's college swimming pool for participants. 'Make this your summer spiritual renewal at the beautiful Hunters Hill campus,' the newspaper invited and three hundred and fifty people turned up.

Imagination and dialogue had replaced the placards and loud speakers of days gone. Noel Rowe taught a course called 'Voices from The Border' the same year as his summer school seminar on poetry. Among the marginal voices were black writing, women's writing, migrant writing and writing about AIDS. A lecturer in English at the University of Sydney and Catholic Theological Union, Rowe's Academy course had some lecture input but its purpose was largely, the outline stated, to encourage a 'sympathetic imagination.' In an interview with Caroline Jones before he left the priesthood, Rowe spoke of the role of imagination and delight. 'We've got to recover the sense of God as pleasure,' he told Jones. He didn't mean sentimentalised pleasure. He was speaking of imagination in sympathy with the margins, the beauty that emerged from hidden swamp places of his childhood memories and symbols.

Rowe had students draw or write their own childhood symbols of landscape, mother and father, or grandmother and grandfather, in his courses on religious imagination that he taught at the Academy and Hunters Hill with Erin White, a former Brigidine sister who did her doctorate in hermeneutics at the University of Sydney. Rowe also taught courses on Christian-Buddhist dialogue with Stephen Fahey, an ex-Marist seminarian who became a Buddhist monk and later ran meditation classes at the Academy under Kevin Bates.

Gerard Hall took Fahey's classes and came back to teach his own course on interfaith and intercultural dialogue after completing his doctorate at Washington's Catholic University of America on the Catalan-Indian Catholic priest, Raimon Panikkar. Hall's interest in Hindu-Christian-Buddhist relations stemmed from his first stint abroad in Washington before visiting Benedictine monk Bede Griffiths's ashram in India and travelling to Sri Lanka and the Philippines en route home. When he returned to Australia after his doctorate he kept in contact with Griffiths and later arranged his visit for an Academy summer school.

Self-esteem and intimacy with God were the topics of the 1994 summer school with Irish Vincentian priest, Pat Collins, a lecturer in spirituality and philosophy at All Hallows' College in Dublin. The flier for the summer school said Collins had worked with the ecumenical movement in Northern Ireland before receiving a call to ministry in 'healing the breaches in the walls of people's spiritual lives.' His book, *Finding Faith in Troubled Times*, dealt with the themes of freedom from fear, deliverance from evil and healing through the sacraments.

Public worship changed key, too, as whole choirs stood up to sing on their wooden boxes. In 1998 the Aquinas Academy sponsored a series of choral interludes at St Patrick's over three Thursday evenings in Lent. The ecumenical, interfaith and culturally diverse programme featured the voices of St Patrick's Chorale, Te Wairua Tapu (Holy Spirit) Maori Choir, a mixed denominational choral group called Mixed Blessings, Sydney Armenian Church Choir, St Mary's Cathedral Choir, Korean Uniting Church Choir, Salvation Army Sydney Congress Hall Songster Brigade and Sydney Jewish Choral Society.

During Kevin's seven-year term as principal the Academy moved from its original buildings on Gloucester Street to Marist Chapel in Circular Quay while St Patrick's was being renovated. The chapel's bare sandstone walls became a lecture hall for the evening courses on spirituality and catechetics. The counselling rooms were turned into office spaces. One night the chapel turned into a jazz club with the jazz musician, Kevin Hunt, accompanying one of the last public talks by the ailing priest from Redfern, Ted Kennedy. It was almost a wake: Kennedy's swansong in a chapel down to a single weekday mass after thirty years of Marist ministry to city commuters. Kevin continued to write and record his songs while he was principal and took his music, like the Christian Growth Programme, to out of the way places in country parishes and city prisons.

'We were founded to be mobile and responsive,' Kevin said. He took up the call literally, living out of his car for much of the decade after he finished at the Academy while completing a second masters at Australian Catholic University. As part of his degree he produced a song cycle on the sacraments, 'Windows to the Sacred.' The disc recording Kevin gave me included a lament for the priesthood. The last stanza, when I listened later in my car, was a cry for truth and love to be seen 'in clearer light:' 'Come the day uncluttered hearts are sharing / given wholly to God's ancient song / Come the day when light bursts from the shadows / and priestly people live where they belong.'

'How does the inspiration come?' I asked Kevin. 'Is it the music first or a song line?'

'I don't even think music. I think of the idea,' he replied. 'My lyric is where I put the energy. The music's just there to support it.'

'So it's through word that it comes.'

'It's like giving birth,' he explained. 'I'll look at a song and think, *Where did you come from?* There's a sense of it having a life of its own.'

'And then having it's own title,' I added.

Kevin has given a French name to the parish restaurant he opened in Hunters Hill, *La Paroisse*. One Friday a month Kevin cooks for his parishioners who share their stories around the presbytery's dining table. One of the more recent guests of *La Paroisse* was Allan Connors. Kevin can now add to his titles an Allan trifecta: chief driver, successor at the Academy and resident chef.

'Is there something that– this is a song line question–' I hesitated.

'Go on.'

'–like a thread that goes through all those years?'

'How do I answer that?' Kevin looked out the window from the presbytery's dining table. 'I suppose it's our Marist thing that's the essence of it, Julie,' he said slowly. 'It's my passion for people on the edge. Where love is God is, I'm there.'

'There's a song in that,' I told him.

'And also I'm passionate about the gospel. I just love God's people, I really do. Father Jean-Claude Colin, our founder, said in one of his one-liners we often quote, *We must build a new church.* He didn't mean to start the church over but to allow the church to become new and young and beautiful again. That would be my song line. And one of his other key influences on me is, *We must always err on the side of mercy and if we can't save people with the law we save them without it.* He had a great respect for the law, but in its place not as overbearing. And that's why I've always felt free to go beyond where the law has allowed us to go. It's a prophetic ministry that we've got and I suppose that's my song line,' he ended. 'Show the face of Jesus in a way that's digestible.'

I asked Tom Ryan about Marist spirituality when I visited the community in Brisbane. Watching them with their five o'clock gin and eating dinner with them each night, I was listening to men listen to each other's stories.

'It's often expressed in terms of a domestic spirituality,' Tom settled back in his armchair after making me a cup of coffee in his flat he took over from John Thornhill, 'a type of ordinariness and at home with the everyday. There's no sense of clericalism.'

'Which was an explicit thing of the founder, Father Colin, wasn't it?' I asked.

'When you think of the highly clericalised post-revolutionary France we were founded to identify with the ordinary diocesan priests and not to try and be any different, as other orders saw themselves, but the ordinary priesthood in touch with the people. It was to be mirrored in manner of dress and way of life. And adding to that domestic, kitchen table thing about us,' Tom went on, 'there's something particularly feminine about it and it's very hard to put words to that. It's more articulated in terms of Mary language. *Be hidden and, as it were, unknown*, Colin said. Be an enabler of others, a facilitator of their gifts.'

Tom's Marist formation in the early sixties was in the same seminary at Greenmeadows in New Zealand where Woodbury was professed at twenty-three. Tom's mother, like Woodbury's, didn't see her son become a priest either. She died of a brain aneurism when Tom was a nineteen-year-old novice. Tom was ordained in 1965 and enrolled in external studies in French and English while teaching at the same boarding school in Silverstream where Woodbury taught after his first heart attack. Three more moves and two university degrees later, Tom took time out from the priesthood for two years when personal issues arose that later he came to see were associated with fear of abandonment triggered by his mother's early death.

'Now I know what it is, it's not such a big deal since others share the same experience and I am more conscious now how it may be at play in my life,' Tom told me. 'It's a part of you, a flaw you can make an asset.'

He came to Australia and eventually rejoined the Marists at Hunters Hill where he spent a summer on a renewal programme with other Marists from Australia and New Zealand. The two-month period of renewal in 1975, like Woodbury's second novitiate between Toongabbie and the Aquinas Academy, was meant to be a time of reflection and re-initiation for what lay ahead. Tom spent the next ten years in parish work in Tasmania then St Patrick's, Church Hill. While he was parish priest at St Patrick's Allan Connors approached him to teach a course in church history at the Academy. After finishing his term at St Patrick's, he completed a licentiate in theology at Weston School of Theology in Boston in the late eighties. He returned to Sydney to work at the Catholic Theological Union and also at the Academy where he taught courses in spirituality, morality, prayer and scriptures that were intended as follow-up courses to the Christian Growth Programme in suburban and regional parishes. In line with his Marist vocation to enable and facilitate other people's gifts, he increasingly developed courses built on real life questions from the floor.

'I'd always allot time for questions,' Tom said. He collected them during the coffee break, in class, and on paper for those who wanted to stay anonymous. 'It was very real for them. They would tend to be mature age, predominantly women, the generation who had grown up before the Second Vatican Council.'

One of Tom's courses, 'A Patchwork of Colours,' explored the neglected books of the New Testament, the letters of Peter, James, Jude, John and the book of Revelation, and addressed questions about anger and intimacy with God, forgiveness, emotions and prayer, and the insights of Jungian psychology and Ignatian spirituality.

Tom stood up to rummage through his filing cabinet for his folder where he had kept a growing list of adult faith questions.

'Here we are, open forum questions,' he sat back down and began to read. 'Questions on the Gulf War, books selling and displaying pornography, experiences of evil, purgatory and indulgences, children and religious experience, prayer and self-absorption, talking to yourself in the presence of God–'

'These were what people were asking in the nineties?'

'These kinds of questions. Depression and being in tune and out of tune with God, what's the difference? Points about the New Age, homosexuality in the church, did miracles stop when Jesus died? Is there a difference between soul and spirit? Can God ever be heard? Mortal sin and serious sin, creation theology, anger and social justice, exorcism, obligation to preserve life, adultery, sex, is the whole of the Old Testament inspired? Getting nowhere in prayer, self-love, acceptance of a situation, how do I find God in my adult children's choices and lifestyles? Did Jesus say forgive and forget?'

'Did you draw on your own experience?' I asked.

'Sometimes, and sometimes I needed time to think about it, or I could only help clarify the question by picking up what might have been underlying it.' He read out a letter from one woman who wrote down her question about unfaith. 'Whenever I get close to God and feel happy in the relationship something from the past is triggered off by a chance saying or thought and it stops me from living the way I want and living close to God. How can this be overcome?'

Barbara Ryan, a mother of eleven children who went along to Academy courses in the eighties and nineties, wrote down her question in a letter to the *Catholic Weekly* in 1991. 'Why when a baby is born do we bathe it, clothe it, wrap it gently and tenderly give it to its mother to feed from the breast?' Barbara was a grandmother in her sixties when she attended the Aquinas Academy, catching the bus to the city from Dee Why each week and sharing insights about forgiveness and acceptance with her adult children. 'When she was supposed to be an old lady,' her eldest daughter, Patricia, told me, 'her mind was young with fresh up to the minute knowledge in which she saw the love of an ever loving ever present God.' Barbara was familiar with grief from her early adulthood. At twenty-three she lost her mother a few weeks after Barbara herself became a mother and saw her brothers come back from the war shell-shocked. Later with her husband she supported struggling new mothers through the Dee Why conference of the St Vincent de Paul Society. A baby is washed, wrapped and suckled, Barbara answered her own question in the columns of the *Catholic Weekly*, 'to save it from suffering the pangs of cold, discomfort and hunger' after surviving birth.

'It was like a third space between the parish and home,' I told Tom after he had read out some more questions. Whether at a mid morning class or a letter to a newspaper editor, real life found a safe passage and place of trust before integrating into the family and community.

'Education is to do with *e-ducere*, you bring it *out* of people not put it *into* people,' Tom explained. 'The word from the Latin is to educe, to bring out, lead out. It's a journey of shared discovery. There is a point to knowing truth for the truth's sake because it's got a beauty and a value in itself. But there's also a point in asking where does it lead? The movement of God and the movement of grace anchors us in the world of relationships and the world outside ourselves, which is what faith is really meant to be.'

After several years fielding a patchwork of questions, Tom went on to teach courses in pastoral theology at the University of Notre Dame in Fremantle using his notes from the Academy. In his late fifties he wrote a doctoral thesis on the moral significance of emotions in Thomas Aquinas and Catholic moral theology. In his early thirties Tom had turned down a scholarship to do a doctorate overseas and taken time off instead from the priesthood. When he returned to academic life, like Celestine Pooley in middle age, he brought with him the fruits of his Marist formation and experience in adult education.

'There's an interesting quote at the end of the code of canon law,' Tom stood up again to pull off a tome from his bookshelf. 'The salvation of souls,' he read, 'is always the supreme law. *Salus animarum suprema lex esto*. I translate that: The supreme law is to bring the mercy of God to people, and to bring people to the mercy of God.'

It could almost have been another Jean-Claude Colin one-liner.

'If you want a summing up of what I think our Marist thing's about,' Tom said, 'that's it.'

Fourteen years after singing his *Magnificat* at the celebration of fifty years of Marist ministry in the Aquinas Academy, Kevin Bates sang for the Marist general chapter in Rome. The song lines born during those days added more threads to the cloth of adult faith questions from a group of vowed men at Mary's table.

'How do we sing the Lord's song / in a land where truth has no home?' 'Can we listen again as our questions begin / to make sense of the gifts that we own?' 'Dare I join in and travel where / the Spirit may be moving?' 'Mary stay with us as we claim / the Spirit's new directing.'

13
Handing On The Faith

Teaching the teachers had been the founding vision of the Aquinas Academy ever since Woodbury's call for 'young men and women of the professions, of the public services, of the various institutions of post-school education, teachers and others' to be formed in the Catholic tradition. Under Thornhill and Connors mothers were added to the list of influencers. When the first graduates in philosophy received their degrees alongside school teachers awarded diplomas in the catechetics course, 'Handing on the Faith,' Woodbury's vision had come full circle after forty years.

Catherine Hammond completed her own circle in education when she was recruited to teach teachers at the Academy. As a young Catholic woman from Vermont aspiring to be a writer in the early fifties, she had joined the Daughters of St Paul in Boston to hand on the faith through books. The order sent her to Boston College in an era when undergraduate women could only enter the schools of nursing or education.

'I was about eighteen, barely out of high school, and next to me in a summer school class was this elderly nun. She must have been, I don't know, *sixty* or more,' Catherine told me, 'and she was in *my* class. She didn't even have a bachelors and she'd been teaching her whole life.'

When she first thought of entering the convent, Catherine was attending the local state school where her father was deputy headmaster. 'I had none of that mystique of wanting to be a nun. At some point in high school I just thought I wanted to do something that was lasting. At that time if you weren't a nun, you couldn't do anything for the church. You couldn't teach in a Catholic school if you weren't a nun. You couldn't even teach first grade.'

She enrolled in English and graduated with high distinction out of two thousand graduates. For her masters thesis she wrote a biography of Boston's Cardinal Cushing, which her order published. She was accepted into a doctoral programme in philosophy at Fordham University and was writing up her doctoral thesis when the order called her back to Boston.

'In those days you didn't question anything. My father nearly had a fit. He couldn't fathom that they would pull me out of a doctoral programme when I was so far along, but see, the order wasn't a teaching order. It was dedicated to writing and publishing and as far as my superiors were concerned I was already qualified to judge manuscripts for publication. So I didn't finish the degree. But it didn't bother me at the time because I was a nun and you just did what—'

'Can I ask how old you were when that happened?' I interrupted Catherine.

'Oh probably in my late twenties,' she sighed. 'I did really well, but I never felt bitter about having to stop. I was happy being a nun.'

She turned to adult education instead, teaching philosophy to novices, writing and editing manuscripts and travelling around the country promoting her order's books, speaking at archdiocesan gatherings of religious educators. Then she was sent to Australia in the years following Vatican II. Women were leaving religious life and communities were disintegrating. Catherine's parents had died before she came to Australia and soon after she arrived her brother died of cancer, leaving her without any family.

'And my religious life, when I needed it to be a family, no longer felt like that. I found that time really hard. I have always said that religious life left me. I didn't leave it.'

After leaving the convent, Catherine found work in the offices of Catholic adult education and media. She had already been teaching one evening a week at the Aquinas Academy while still a nun and continued her classes in the history of philosophy and the philosophy of the human person. Two of her students were Aloysius Rego and Celestine Pooley.

'The first rush of nuns were free to get out and take courses. They were everywhere. They were having a ball!'

She taught mothers and fathers as well as non-Catholics and non-believers with real life questions. 'The people who went to Aquinas were really keen. I remember one guy with six kids holding down two jobs attending my evening classes. He always asked challenging questions.'

Catherine also taught catechetics to student teachers learning the sacraments.

'For me, Aquinas was a friendly, stimulating place to be,' Catherine said. 'It was a spiritual home. I hadn't had that at uni. We were an almost cloistered order so after classes, I went straight back to the convent. In a way Aquinas was like the campus I never had.'

Catherine dated some of her older students, one of whom was Sam Hammond who had attended classes with Woodbury. They married a few years later in Marist Chapel and Catherine went back to full time publishing. She was headhunted by Doubleday and later became managing editor for a family-run Catholic press, EJ Dwyer. More recently she freelanced as an editor and writing teacher while also giving occasional courses at the Aquinas Academy. One of her courses in 2006 was on 'The Psychology of Home.'

'You must have a huge amount of resilience,' I told Catherine and she laughed. 'I mean, leaving the convent wasn't the first thing you'd had to adapt to. You'd already had to leave your doctorate,' I was still circling what happened before she lost her whole family and community.

'Yes, but I have never regretted my years as a nun, Julie, nor having to start out on my own at mid life. I made those decisions. Nobody forced me. I took those vows freely. I knew what they were. And then changes came, the church changed, religious life changed. Everything changed. And my life changed. I'm grateful for it all and I hope I've done some good.'

Forty students received their two-year diplomas and another thirty-nine got certificates for 'Handing on the Faith,' the *Catholic Weekly* reported at the end of 1990. Bishop David Cremin presented the awards at a graduation mass at St Patrick's. 'There is great hope for Catholic education,' the programme coordinator, Brother Pius Jones, said in his address to the students. 'If our parishes and schools have teachers like you, then we have a positive future ahead. We are seeing a larger number of young people with a very strong faith commitment, eager to pass this commitment on.'

Catherine Jordan travelled into the city from Macquarie University with two other students to attend the course. Catherine was studying economics and audited the course out of interest. Her two friends living at the same university college were training to be teachers and completed the certificate as a requirement for teaching religion. They were committed young people eager to share their faith, walking to Sunday mass together and catching the bus to Wynyard one evening a week to study scripture and doctrine. 'We sat down the front and another person who sat down the front with us was a mature age student called Stephen Reeves. During the course we got to know him better, and we'd normally sip our coffees with him during break time. It was during one of those break times, at least half way into the course, that he bravely opened up and said he thought that God might be calling him to the priesthood. We encouraged him to test out that calling. He did that and not too long afterwards entered the seminary at Kensington as a mature age student.' Stephen was later ordained in the Wollongong diocese.

Religious education changed name and content according to staffing and tertiary requirements. Gerard Hall helped run the catechetics programme in the mid eighties before he left for his doctoral studies in Washington. Two Marists, Robert Hollow and Pius Jones, were appointed to assist Allan Connors with the Christian Growth Programme, help with summer schools, look after finances and run the Academy bookshop where books were always laid out with biscuits and cups for visitors dropping by. Coordination of the catechetics course fell to Pius Jones, then a lay theologian, Matthew Ogilvie, then Hall again after his return to Australia to teach at the Catholic Theological Union. Finally another Marist, Luke Holohan, who had completed his doctorate at Trinity College, Dublin, took it over in 1999. The two-year certificate offered in the city and at Blacktown included courses in church history, sacraments, Christian and Jewish scriptures, Christian life and ethics, faith and theology, religious education, liturgy and pastoral care and incorporated a two-day retreat for participants. The certificate was eventually closed down as teachers opted out of the programme in favour of cheaper and less intensive in-house accreditation through the Catholic schools office or upgrading to a university masters programme.

A foundations certificate in systematic theology tried to tap a broader constituency. The twelve-month course was developed by the Institute of Faith Education in Brisbane and taught at the Aquinas Academy as stage one of a three-stage programme. Designed for teachers, nurses, social workers, parish ministers and others whose interest was not necessarily vocational, it included topics on the Old Testament, church history, liturgy and sacraments, God's self-communication in Christ and the Christian way of life.

At the end of 1998 the population of Hunters Hill seminary was down as numbers seeking ordination diminished and theological education turned mainstream amid the expansion of Catholic multi-campus tertiary institutions, such as Notre Dame and Australian Catholic University. Two national reviews of adult faith education in the nineties commissioned by the National Catholic Education Commission and the Queensland bishops boiled down to a question: was there a difference between faith 'education' and faith 'formation'? One review said no; faith education encompassed university departments, parish groups, retreats and pastoral training in the dioceses. One said yes, sometimes. The Aquinas Academy did both and accreditation had been its goal ever since Woodbury's speech about rats in Sydney. Education (more or less) emphasised outcomes. Formation (more or less) focused on process. It was the same creative tension Tom Ryan outlined in his 1984 homily, the same tension between action and contemplation in the church. Both were needful or there'd be no bread.

A single white pearl lay in the lap of a Swarovski crystal shell on the sidepiece of Marie Biddle's living room where we talked about her faith influencers. It was a gift for Marie's fifty years as a Sister of St Joseph. The pearl of great price was a symbol handed on from her grandmother, who as a young girl accompanied Mary MacKillop to the halfway bridge between Glen Innes and Inverell more than half a century before Marie struggled with the idea that God might be calling her to be a nun.

'My great-grandmother had a hotel in Glen Innes and she offered to get a transport for Mary MacKillop when she was on visitation of the nuns. My grandmother and her brother took Mary MacKillop to the halfway bridge and another family from Inverell came and picked her up from there.'

Marie and her parents were taught by Josephites at Glen Innes and Marie's mother followed her great-grandmother's example, transporting the nuns and taking them on picnics. One day when Marie was sent over from the school to the convent next door she happened to meet the mother general, who asked if she wanted to be a nun.

'I said, *No thanks, Sister, I couldn't bear wearing all that clobber you people wear.* Mum was coming to pick her up and as I put her in the car she said, *Well I'll pray for you.* And I said, *Well don't pray too hard because I don't want it.* But it was there in the back of my mind,' Marie told me. 'And when I finished the leaving certificate I thought if I did teaching at least it's sort of on the way. I'm not dodging God completely.'

She got a scholarship to Armidale teachers' college and boarded in a student house run by Ursuline sisters. She liked the other students and her classes but was having trouble dodging God. 'I failed a course, which jolted me because I'd never failed anything in my life,' Marie said. 'But I remember sitting in that class writing rubbish and I knew this fail was telling me, *This isn't you.*'

She went home to Glen Innes and decided to go down to Sydney and ask the convent to let her get in and get out and get the nun thing over and done with. Mother Leonie told her, 'We don't want you if you don't want to come, dear.'

'And I thought they'd be there with open arms,' Marie said. 'I cried, *Please let me come in. I've been trying to get over this thing and I just want to get on with life.*'

Mother Leonie gave in with a knowing smile and sent Marie crying in the rain in a car to her aunt's house in Kensington. Marie entered the convent in Baulkham Hills as a postulant on 12 January 1962. 'And it had on the calendar that day, *So Jesus began his miracles,*' she recalled.

Postulants were sent out to communities to live for a year and teach in schools before starting the two-year novitiate. Marie was eighteen, teaching sixty-four wriggly primaries in Beverly Hills and still trying to dodge God. When she began her novitiate she asked the novice mistress to let her know if she didn't think she belonged. The novice mistress told her she couldn't pass on the buck.

'So she was putting the discernment back to you?' I asked Marie.

'Absolutely. But the reality was that was unusual those days. Once you put your hand to the plough you didn't put it back. I can remember one time as a postulant,' her voice softened, 'looking out the window and thinking, *The train's just down there. If you don't want to stay you can easily go home.* But I knew I had to be convinced. Just before my profession the novice mistress said, *Have you made up your mind?* And I said, *I've got no reason not to stay*.'

She was professed on 6 January 1965, the year *Perfectae Caritatis*, Pope Paul VI's decree on the adaptation and renewal of religious life, sent some religious communities packing and others soul searching following Vatican II. The decree stipulated that religious superiors attend to the spiritual and intellectual formation of their members: 'Adaptation and renewal depend greatly on the education of religious,' it stated. 'Neither non-clerical religious nor religious women should be assigned to apostolic works immediately after the novitiate. Rather, their religious and apostolic formation, joined with instruction in arts and science directed toward obtaining appropriate degrees, must be continued as needs require in houses established for those purposes.'

Like Catherine Hammond, Marie had the benefit of a formation that hadn't been available to older generations of women religious. In the lecture rooms of the Mount Street secondary teachers' training college Marie sat next to members of other congregations gleaning the new approach to religious life. One of her lecturers in the novitiate was Roger Pryke, the university chaplain and thorn in Woodbury's side. Pryke already ran a formation course for nuns at Sancta Sophia college where he encouraged questions and discussion, introduced psychoanalysis and showed films by the French director, Roger Bresson, whose 1951 *Diary of a Country Priest* was made from the earlier Georges Bernanos novel banned in Sydney's seminary. At Lewisham he gave weekly lectures on the Old Testament and psalms to the Little Company of Mary and at Baulkham Hills he cast flame into the hearts of young Josephite novices. 'Set pools of silence in this thirsty land,' Marie recited the line from James McAuley that drew her to something she had struggled to name more than fifty years earlier in her search for her vocation.

I mentioned to Marie a Max Dupain photograph of nuns on Newport Beach. She got out her albums to show me photos of the day she entered Baulkham Hills as a postulant and on her profession day in full habit. After Vatican II the veil was simplified and hemlines went up like school uniforms in the sixties. One photo showed Marie in mock strangle of a sheepish teenage girl trying to cover her hem with her schoolbooks.

After over a decade teaching in high schools Marie took a year off to finish her degree at Armidale. There she discovered that religion was what she wanted to teach more than anything else. She led small co-educational classes in Bankstown using sixteen-year-old questions about faith and unfaith as the curriculum. Like Tom Ryan's open forum discussions, Marie was facilitating adult faith education in the classroom. Her provincial told her, like Kevin Bates, to go and find something overseas. Marie picked a masters in formative spirituality at Duquesne University in Pittsburgh where she could begin to integrate insights from experience, psychology and theology. After only one year of full time study at university since entering the convent, Marie left her veil and Josephite community in her mid thirties to join a class of international students under the Dutch priest and psychologist, Adrian van Kaam.

'I became a nun over there, I think,' Marie explained. 'I mean, I was a nun, but I got a real sense of what it was to be a Josephite because I was out of the context and I knew what was common to us. But the other thing was that I really got a sense of vocation there because for the first time it made me realise what a vocation is. You choose a context to be who you are.'

Another van Kaam student from Australia, Michael Whelan, had finished the masters programme before Marie and was back for his doctorate. Marie asked him what she'd struggled with since Mother Leonie had sent her home crying in the rain at eighteen.

'How do you tell what God wants you to be?'

'You don't,' Michael said. 'You and God have to work it together.'

'So many people *wanted* to be nuns,' Marie went on, 'and this is what I couldn't understand in the novitiate. They all wanted to be and then they were going. And I was the one who was struggling to want to be and here I was staying.'

Van Kaam passed on to his students what he'd learnt as a seminarian during the Nazi occupation of Holland, surviving on turnips while smuggling food to Jews in hiding. He held classes on adult faith in postwar factories before coming to America to study psychology and setting up his programme in formative spirituality. Marie took classes in scripture, sacramental theology and the spiritual classics filtered through the fields of life formation. Her second year incorporated spiritual direction with a clinical dose of neurolinguistics.

'The limits of your language are the limits of your mind,' Marie quoted Austrian philosopher Ludwig Wittgenstein, one of the 'Oxford-style linguistic analysts' Woodbury's Dominican offsider, Reginald Batten, had disparaged in writing to fellow Irish Dominican Cardinal Browne. 'The structure of your language is the structure of your psyche,' Marie joined French analyst, Jacques Lacan, to the Oxford group. The psychologists who taught spiritual direction told Marie's class to 'listen for the deletions, the distortions and the generalisations' because they held the key to the infraconscious where shadows of trauma and the transcendent moved under the surface of the deep. However Oxford-style linguistic analysis named it, where silent pain was hidden there was a silent God waiting to be met.

Van Kaam confirmed Marie's intuition that handing on the faith was not about teaching people to be Christians, but helping them become human. 'The thing from the Catholic point of view that I was resisting, it was an intuitive resistance from my childhood I think, that outside the church there's no salvation. Why would God who loves everybody do that? That's not to decry Christ,' she added. 'Christ revealed our humanity, but we must know our humanity if we're going to be able to go beyond our own little structure. Christ came via Jewish tradition to tell *all* nations that life comes in lovingly facing death.'

One of van Kaam's Dutch Jewish contemporaries, Etty Hillesum, had also learnt what it was to become human during the war. While studying foreign languages and learning to pray on her bathroom floor watching bombs fall outside her window, Etty asked in her late twenties, 'Why is there a war?' She answered her own adult question before she was murdered at Auschwitz: 'Because I and my neighbour and everyone else do not have enough love.'

After returning from Pittsburgh Marie was appointed to teach spirituality to seminarians at a time when the church looked with suspicion on women spiritual directors in seminaries. Leading retreats and prayer days for her own congregation was one thing; introducing Flannery O'Connor to aspiring priests through the lens of their own life experience was another. She could be called a formative director, but spiritual direction was best left to the traditional domain of ordained men.

'I felt like I was punch drunk. I couldn't fix this,' Marie said. This time she couldn't talk her way through her struggle. She couldn't break the confidentiality of her directees by explaining what was really happening in formative and spiritual direction. Instead she wrote her way through the impasse, using Constance FitzGerald's work as the basis of a masters thesis in theology on 'learning to live more creatively within the limits of a human system.' She completed her thesis at the Catholic Theological Union under the supervision of Michael Whelan and taught with him courses on human and Christian formation, spiritual growth processes and the spiritual classics.

When Whelan became the new principal of the Aquinas Academy in 2000 Marie was appointed convenor of programmes and facilitated a four-unit course, 'Developing Your Own Spirituality.' Over the past sixteen years she has taught the classics of spirituality, film, religious poetry, contemporary women mystics and led retreats and reflection days with Michael at Kincumber, Baulkham Hills and Colo.

'I don't see myself primarily as a presenter,' Marie said. 'I'd much rather be the spiritual director and I think I'm a good supporter and a facilitator and it's good for Michael to have the backing of someone who knows where he's going. Don't try to be the head,' Marie's mother used to tell her. 'Just try and be the neck and point the head in the right direction.'

I asked her about the changes she'd seen in sixteen years and she went quiet.

'I just feel it's been–' she stopped to face me. 'The work's not the main thing. The relationships have been the main thing. A lot of it was companionship,' she summed up her gift. Like her grandmother accompanying someone to a halfway bridge where another comes to take her place.

14
A Mystical Heart

The course reader for 'Developing Your Own Spirituality' included an article by American theologian Charles Davis called 'A Hidden God.' Michael Whelan first read it in 1972, the year he was ordained, and has been sprinkling it like salt ever since. 'The busier we are about liturgical matters, the lay apostolate, ecumenism, the biblical revival, reform of Church structures and all the rest,' Davis wrote in 1966, 'the less need there is to confront the reality of God in our own lives. We are covering over the void in our own hearts. A fear prevents us from admitting the emptiness we should find there. We must face that emptiness,' Davis went on, 'because it is the presence of God calling us.' On those prepared to meet this hidden God in the silent dark, Davis said, 'the solid work of renewal depends.'

A year after Vatican II, Davis saw what Sandra Schneiders later described as the spiritual fragmentation of a system trying to put itself together again after knocking Thomism from its high wall and pretending not to notice the empty space. For a twenty-five-year-old straight out of seminary, didn't it scare the hell out of him helping God's people?

Michael had been thrown into the psychological deep end at Marist Chapel seeing people with real life experiences he'd never personally faced, some in grave distress. A confrère invited him to try a charismatic prayer group. 'It was in one of those row houses at Redfern. Abbot Hawkins, a Trappist monk, used to pray there. I'd pick up one of the elderly Josephite nuns from St Margaret's hospital and we'd go over. She always sat in the back seat!' Michael recalled her convent manners. 'But that was my opening up into contemplative prayer and a much richer reading of the sacred scriptures.'

In his eight years in seminary Michael had read Marx's communist manifesto but had never been taught to face the void in his own heart. Instead he was given 'head and teeth spirituality. You got all this abstract information under the heading of mystical and ascetical theology, about humility as Teresa of Ávila understood it, for example, but it wasn't formative.' After a few years practising discursive meditation according to the first week of Saint Ignatius's spiritual exercises, he went to see his spiritual director. 'Prayer for me was just sheer drudgery,' Michael said. 'Some instinct in me, maybe a cry for help, said to him, *I think I'm being called to a higher form of prayer. And he said, No, keep doing the meditation.*' Contemplative prayer, the place of the void, was more dangerous than Marx for a twenty-two-year-old seminarian.

Around the same time he was warned off mysticism Michael and forty other seminarians were bussed into the city to hear the Spanish master general of the Dominicans speak on Saint Thomas at the Aquinas Academy. It was Woodbury's shining moment in the Thomist spotlight. 'After it was over we were standing out on the footpath in Gloucester Street. John Jago, who had just been ordained, came over, feigned inspection of the gutter and said, *Any minute the pure milk of Thomism will come flowing down*.'

I burst out laughing at the sheer audacity. Jack Soulsby, fifteen years older than his fellow seminarians, told me it was more like whisky.

'It was the end-time of neo-scholasticism that had been taught in seminaries throughout the Catholic world for generations,' Michael explained. 'John Thornhill was taking us out of that, but Wilf Radford was firmly ensconced in that way of thinking.'

It was John Thornhill who introduced the communist manifesto in class. When he became principal of the Aquinas Academy he introduced students to the charismatic movement with a series of lectures on the gifts of the Holy Spirit and the miraculous in prayer meetings. Charismatic renewal wasn't to be feared, Thornhill told the *Catholic Weekly*. It was part of a pattern in the church's history. As chaplain to a charismatic group, he said 'I have become convinced that God's grace is working among them.' Personal experiences of prayer tended not to be a group event for Catholics, 'but in their simplicity of faith and sharing of their faith, charismatics display a trust and a loving, simple atmosphere of participation. It is another form of demonstration of the Mystical Body of Christ.'

The simple and the miraculous were flowing down Redfern for a devout Trappist monk, an old-school Josephite and a young Marist priest learning to pray. 'We'd sing hymns, sometimes people would pray in tongues, sometimes someone would ask for prayer so they'd kneel in the middle–'

'Like healing?' I asked Michael.

'Healing, whatever. Someone would lead it but it was very freewheeling à la the Pentecostal movement. It was a great transition for me,' Michael said. 'It broke down a lot of barriers and opened up some wellsprings inside me, a love of the scripture and an ability to read the scriptures in a way other than academic and a way of praying other than discursive meditation. One of the structures that came out of the charismatic prayer meeting was to sit in a group together for three hours. The first hour you took a scriptural text, which you all agreed upon, and you just sat with it in silence and you did a *lectio divina*. The second hour you wrote about it, a *meditatio*, and then the third hour you shared.'

Michael helped bring the movement to Tasmania where he taught high school for four and a half years. When he left for postgraduate study in Pittsburgh he attended a group for a while but the wellsprings were opening elsewhere. He'd found new tools and words to reach the places of unfaith in his life.

The five years in Pittsburgh brought him to a cliff edge. He had read pieces of Adrian van Kaam's *Religion and Personality* in seminary but it wasn't until 1981 when Michael went back to Duquesne University for his doctorate that it became deeply and concretely personal.

'Van Kaam insisted that to do a doctorate you had to base your research on an event you had lived through. In the sixties he introduced to the English-speaking world the personalist psychology along the phenomenological line that was already happening in Europe. It's a marvellous, very rich way of thinking. So you took an event and there were protocols for examining it and giving it some kind of inter-subjective validity.'

'An event from childhood?' I asked.

'Well actually the event I took happened in 1977 when I went through Mexico City on my way to van Kaam for my masters. It was a crisis for me. Quite a huge, wonderful crisis as it turned out, but terribly disorientating and painful. I spent a year picking it over and letting other people observe it, trying to get to the fundamental dynamics of what actually happened. Then I researched it in terms of its component parts. Van Kaam demanded that we leave religion right out of the picture to begin with, any religion, and look at the universal human dimension. So I went to psychologists, sociologists, philosophers and novelists. The universal human dimension led into the universal religious dimension and I had to examine it from the point of view of a religious tradition other than my own. So I used Zen Buddhism. Then thirdly I researched it from a Christian view and in the fourth level I looked at it from the point of view of a selected population, which for me was Roman Catholic priests. It was just wonderful, at times extremely trying, but in the end it gave me a way of thinking that is very creative and enriching because it won't allow me to stray from experience, from what's actually happening, what's real.'

The huge, painful, disorientating life event that hit Michael in Mexico City at thirty led to a crisis of vocation. Five years later, while Michael was in the middle of his doctoral studies, he visited another Marist priest in Chicago. They talked and talked in his car. He'd been ordained in 1963, nine years ahead of Michael, just before Thomism fell off its high wall. He was teaching in a Marist school when the papal encyclical *Humanae vitae* came out and God's people told him in the confessional and at their dining tables, *I don't believe that anymore.* He went to the missions and ended up in Chicago in search of a new apologetic. Later he stopped his studies and left the ministry.

'My path could have been the same had I gotten into academic philosophy,' Michael said. 'I hate to think what would have happened. Doing my doctorate I was actually putting my life together. It just hit me one day, *Why did you become a priest?* I had never really critically examined my motivation. I turned up at the seminary and just kept going.'

'And no one asked you at the seminary?'

'Nobody asked me and I don't think they would have been competent to deal with it. The first question that came to me was, *Did I do it to get away from life?* And I let it swing for however long it was going to have to swing. I had made up my mind I would go if that's where the pennies landed. But it was in that car in Chicago–'

'You knew you belonged.' I finished. I wondered what made one and not the other stay. Was it the miraculous in a prayer meeting, or Zen Buddhism or a Dutch priest who had learnt how to be human in a war?

I asked Michael about an icon of Mary behind him on the wall of his office where we were talking. I recognised it as the Russian icon of *Umileniye*, sometimes translated as Loving Kindness, depicting the child Wisdom pressed close to the face of tenderness: an image of grief turned into courage. I wondered how it spoke to Michael's vocation.

'How do you describe love?' he asked. 'How do you describe intimacy? How do you describe joy? When you get down to that level you've got to use metaphors and similes. I don't say the rosary anymore, but the rosary for me was a means to an end. I don't have any particular devotions to Mary. I do pray to her. Colin said, *You're a Marist by a most gracious choice.* I take that very seriously. I was chosen. So that's part of my daily prayer. But he also said, and we've got it in our constitutions, *You have to learn to breathe like Mary.*'

'Wow.'

'That's a metaphor. It's a way of presence. I love Heidegger's definition of allowing things to be present as they are in them–' Michael went back to the phenomenologists. 'I did this bloody postgraduate course on Being and Time,' he reached for Heidegger on the shelf. '*Sein und Zeit.*'

'Sounds better in German!' I said.

'Thus phenomenology means to let that which shows itself be seen from itself in the very way in which it shows itself from itself,' he read in a circle. 'It's this whole idea of showing. Things are capable of radiating light and being an epiphany in other words. It's like, you know those pictures, kids have them, where if you look at it in a certain way, *Oh now I see it!*'

'Like a hologram?'

'That sort of thing. There has to be a quieting of oneself in order to let the other–' he turned the picture again. 'I remember Maurice Friedman talking about Buber and how important the in-between is. To allow the in-between to happen is to allow the other and yourself to come to that point and it's not by effort, by intelligence or talent. It's by grace.'

In the end it didn't matter whether it was the charismatics, or Zen Buddhism, or Heidegger's hologram or Buber's in-between that taught Michael to breathe like Mary. It was all grace anyway.

The first time I heard Michael Whelan describe love was in a circle of mainly middle-aged women who had turned up for a four-week course on forgiveness as part of a 'Contemplative Rhythm' series he taught with Marie Biddle. I had found the leaflet, most probably yellow, at the back of St Patrick's one day in the city and read that the course would show a film based on a true story of a woman in a remote village in Iran after the Islamic revolution who was falsely accused of adultery by her husband and was stoned to death. I don't remember how love entered the circle of anger, shame and forgiveness but I remember Michael used two forefingers like puppets to meet in the middle and said, *Mary loves Joseph to make Joseph more Joseph, and Joseph loves Mary to make Mary more Mary*. When the puppet play was over one woman sighed, *Oh to have that, Michael*. I wrote the play down in my journal afterwards.

Before watching the film we had a week to reflect on the gospel story of Jesus using his forefinger to write in the dust at the feet of those who judged another. We were given a prayer, scripture, *lectio divina* and contemplative exercise for each of the twenty-eight days and time for sharing each week, like the third hour of a charismatic prayer meeting. After watching the film we had a discussion. The character that affected me wasn't the condemned woman, but her older relative who brushed her hair, sung to her, dressed her and walked with her, holding her the whole way to her death. It was the woman accompanying another. Michael had to leave early in time for a bible study with judges in the supreme court. Marie led the rest of us in stillness and played a Celtic blessing of peace as we left fifteen minutes later. I walked quickly from class and looked up suddenly to see Michael, on the other side of King Street, approaching the court half an hour after our discussion had ended. I stopped and watched his slow rhythm. He must have been breathing in between each step.

In 2005 Esther de Waal, an internationally known Anglican lay woman teacher, writer and retreat-giver in the Benedictine tradition, delivered a lecture at the Aquinas Academy on the topic, 'Living with a Monastic Heart Today.' It was part of a series of diamond jubilee lectures that were published and dedicated to Austin Woodbury 'and all those who joined in the work of adult education through the Aquinas Academy over the sixty years, 1945-2005.' The lecture topics ranged, like the Academy's own life cycle, from natural law, ethics, interfaith dialogue, Vatican II, monastic spirituality, theology as conversation, church structures and spiritual freedom. De Waal began her talk with the image of a bell calling people to be awake. Like learning to breathe, contemplative living was a way of being present in a world asleep with overactivity.

The following year, American Franciscan Richard Rohr was one of the invited international speakers at the Academy. It was his third visit to Australia and he was hosted off church property. His itinerary was spread between three cities and included two public lectures, two retreat days, a day for school principals and a weekend retreat. There were public lectures in three cities when the archbishop of Westminister, Cardinal Cormac Murphy-O'Connor, came out the same year at the invitation of the Aquinas Academy. Distinguished international speakers kept coming with an afternoon at the Sydney town hall in 2013 for the visit of former Irish president, Mary McAleese, co-hosted by Catalyst for Renewal, an organisation founded for dialogue in the church that has held an annual series of reflection mornings in partnership with the Aquinas Academy. Cross-fertilisation and collaboration within and without church structures was also a strategy of living in between.

'My conviction grows,' Michael told me, 'that the renewal of the church depends on a recovery of the contemplative and the mystical dimension. It's not the recovery of doctrine. The mystical heart of the church is what has to be inflamed. We've got to teach people how to be mystics, how to be contemplative. We need to teach theology. We need to teach good thinking. We need to keep the law. All that, yes yes yes yes, a thousand times yes. But none of that's going to be worth anything if the mystical heart is not alive.'

It was almost as if the flow of sixty years asking *what* to live had dried up in the heart teaching the body *how* by facing the void in between each breath. Constance FitzGerald summed up the prophetic call from impasse to hope in a 2009 article on the crisis of memory. Twenty-five years after she had called for a spirituality of suffering, violation and dying, she probed deeper the mystical tradition of forgetting. Addressing a group of American theologians FitzGerald described the purification of memory, according to Saint John of the Cross, as an unravelling of the threads of the past when meaning and identity were no longer found in what went before. The intellectual and institutional imperative *not* to forget, not to silence the voiceless, FitzGerald said, was a creative tension with the mystical and contemplative imperative *not* to remember, to face the void in silence. It was a prophetic call, a graced work of dispossession, to leave behind the fragments of an irrecoverable past for the sake of recovering hope. 'Those who finally understand and give their lives over to the dismantling of the archives of memory by accepting the gift of hope eschew keeping a death grip on what has given them assurance of their value and place in the Church.'

I asked Michael about the sacrament of solitude he had mentioned in a recent seminar on Thomas Merton, the Trappist monk born in France a year and two weeks after Etty Hillesum was born in Holland. I thought maybe there might be a sacrament of forgetting. In 1952 Merton wrote: 'Have the people of our age acquired a Midas touch of their own, so that as soon as they succeed, everything they touch becomes crowded with people?' Eight years later he wrote: 'Once God has called you to solitude, everything you touch leads you further into solitude.' Both success and solitude sounded contagious.

'To me the essence of sacrament is that you find the divine in the human, the finite in the infinite,' Michael answered my question touching his finger tips in an arc, 'meeting in the one place, in the one thing,' he clapped his palms flat against each other. 'And I would speak of loneliness as a sacrament, too. I think it's a step and if you ricochet off it and run into something to escape you miss the sacramentality of it all. But if you listen and you face it you move very quickly, I think, into the realisation of your aloneness, even if you don't call it that.'

'It's one sacrament leading to another sacrament,' I responded.

'Indeed. And it's an opening into the infinite through the finite,' he said. 'It just keeps expanding. Our hearts are made for that so we want more of it.'

When Michael was seven Pope Pius XII canonised Peter Chanel, a Marist missionary martyred in the Pacific. Michael's grandmother lived opposite the Hunters Hill grounds where some of the first French Marist missionaries were buried and she used to save the *Harvest* magazine published by the Australian province of the Society of Mary. Maybe it was from his grandmother's collection of *Harvest* stories about Saint Peter Chanel, or the legends his father Brian relayed about an old classmate shot down over Germany in the war who went on to become a Marist priest, that Michael caught something contagious. Later he got to know the Marist priests from Lismore who came and said mass at Wardell where Michael's family lived. There were only, Michael quoted TS Eliot, 'hints and guesses' of what was to come. 'The hint half guessed, the gift half understood,' Eliot said, 'is Incarnation.'

Michael's mother, Dympna, was one of the mature age students who came to the Aquinas Academy in the years following Vatican II. She and Brian moved to Sydney while Michael was completing his doctorate in Pittsburgh. Dympna Whelan sat in the front row of classes given by Catherine Hammond and Tom Ryan. She'd never had any tertiary education and there wasn't time for books with thirteen children. When Michael was four his mother had mumps when she was pregnant with her seventh child. Martin lived for eleven months and died the year Michael began school.

'I have vague memories of him in the cot,' Michael said. 'He couldn't eat, couldn't focus his eyes, he couldn't even cry properly. The brain hadn't developed.'

I asked Michael about the impact of his mother's real life experience on her faith education at the Academy.

'It had a huge impact on her and, you know, I never talked to Mum about that. Or not in any great deal. She was very thoughtful and in a good sense critical, questioning. She didn't just take it in. She certainly was not a law and order type Catholic. It was the Spirit, the contemplative thing, that really attracted her. It wasn't answers she was after. She was searching. There was a depth there that you couldn't satisfy with answers or theories. And sometimes I'd say things from theology,' I imagined him holding up a Heidegger hologram or speaking in Buber to her, 'and she'd say, *I don't know what you're talking about.*'

Even if she didn't understand his words, maybe it was from her he caught how to face the void in his heart.

15
Nazareth

Twelve years after classes for adult faith commenced in wartime Woodbury circulated a memorandum to the provincial explaining the pattern of slipping enrollments. There was a drop in tertiary-age students and retention rates fell during the year. The lack of an accredited outcome, the rising cost of transport to the city and the disparity of knowledge between older and newer students had contributed to the waning interest, Woodbury said. There was also increasing competition with television. The full-page *Catholic Weekly* advertisements featuring young, attractive, smiling, coffee-sipping, male and female students watching the white dust coat wildly gesticulating at the blackboard with cartoon facial expressions, were a decoy against cold nights at home on the couch. The advertisements worked for a time: enrollments peaked at over six hundred in 1962, but had halved by the mid sixties and fizzled out to a few dozen by the time of Woodbury's forced retirement at the end of 1974.

After the diamond jubilee celebrations Whelan noted in his annual report for the provincial the changing demographics of adult faith education. Listing the twenty-five regular courses held throughout the year, including nine offered in the city and Blacktown as part of the final year of the certificate in religious studies, Whelan concluded with a comment on the 'privatization' and 'multiplication' of life and faith with the result that clientele had shrunk over two generations. Where thirty thousand had turned up in the rain to watch a Catholic apologist debate a Communist apparatchik in a Sydney stadium during the blockade of Berlin, three thousand gathered on a windy night in Sydney's town hall to hear a statement from Rome on the eve of a new millennium. For their respective eras the numbers on both occasions were impressive but unrepeatable.

'That group of Catholics who grew up in the pre-Vatican II Church and wanted to understand their Catholicism and the Church in which they had been inculturated,' Whelan referred to his mother's generation, 'has substantially and rapidly diminished.' In Dympna Whelan's time Academy courses attracted up to two thousand enrollments a year not including weekend workshops, seminars and summer schools. Subsequent annual reports added that the number of quality presenters had markedly declined. Participants also had growing care responsibilities for grandchildren and were more likely to attend a one-off event like a Richard Rohr or a reflection morning. Annual figures in 2010 to 2013 were less than two hundred with a spike in evening courses offered in 2013 on Thomas Merton and 'The Way of Silent Presence'—a short course based on the *Cloud of Unknowing*. A mystical heart calling the church to keep awake or a flash in the pan never to be seen again once the Merton centenary died down and people went back to being crowded?

'It is time to establish a Marist community at Nazareth,' Whelan ended his 2011 report. Two years later the provincial administration declined a proposal to extend the property acquired in 2007 on the Colo River. What could come of Nazareth?

I'd heard from Wiradjuri woman and poet Maisie Cavanagh that Nazareth was the start of a love story. Deerubbin became lonely after a lifetime flowing and forming the land. When a magpie told him about the river travelling from the northwest he wanted to meet her. She was called Colo and she'd lost her direction. Seeing in the eyes of a kookaburra the river coming from the southwest she said *Yes* to the kookaburra and, receiving her new name, flowed into the wide deep waters of Deerubbin to make their way together toward the sea.

The fertile banks were invaded and stripped and blood flowed from the land's wound. Across the ocean another war had taken away the children's bread. Wasn't it time, a man asked, that the children had a mother again? A mother to be with God and alone and with friend, making her needs one with God's children so they could be fed. 'Having once tasted God,' Jean-Claude Colin said, 'everything else would take care of itself.' He wrote down what he saw. 'I place myself in the home of Nazareth, and from there I see all that I have to do.' Colin saw Nazareth as a sign of the mystical heart of the church.

'My experience over more than forty years within the Society,' Whelan wrote to his provincial four decades after being weaned with nothing solid to taste, 'is that Father Colin's vision for us to value solitude and silence has been largely overlooked.' Returning from Pittsburgh with renewed vocation he had started to search, on and off for twenty years in rural estate, with the half-hearted hope one day of fulfilling Colin's vision. Soon Whelan would be turning sixty. Perhaps it was time, whispered the provincial after the diamond jubilee, that the Aquinas Academy left its own precious gem for the generations to come. Within a year, sixty acres on the banks of the Colo were sighted off Putty Road. *Yes,* said the council. *Now go out and do it.* News travelled from Rome, on the name feast of Mary, in favour of Nazareth. Mary smiled on her home, all the saints gave thanks, and an ancient song rose for the magpie and the kookaburra to make truth and mercy meet again.

The bishop and the elder came to bless the land. 'We acknowledge the Darug people, the original inhabitants of this land,' said one and the other welcomed with smoke all who were there.

'We gather here today to bless a place set aside for those who desire solitude and silence in order to nourish their relationship with God,' the bishop began. 'Our indigenous ancestors, as they walked this land for millennia, spoke of *dadirri*, deep listening. We seek to hear your Word with the ear of the heart in this place of solitude and silence.'

And the word was read by a woman. 'Come away to a deserted place all by yourselves and rest a while,' Jesus invited. 'And they went away in the boat to a deserted place by themselves.'

The right hand touched the water in the name of the three to birth an ancient gift, to wash and suckle with goodness and truth. And all said *Amen* and were blessed.

Like Nazareth of old, there was a working shed with a place for guests and a small home where the holy family had dwelt. A traveller in the land gave her name to the home.

'Mary MacKillop reminds us, *We are but travellers here,*' spoke one whose grandmother had travelled to a halfway bridge. In silence the travellers drew near to the memory of another young traveller in the land.

'Bless this icon,' prayed the bishop. 'Let it awaken your Presence in the minds and hearts of those who come into its presence. May those who seek courage and discernment through Mary MacKillop's intercession, find it in this place,' he finished by sprinkling the icon with waters of grace.

'The Lord be with you,' the bishop turned to face the people again. 'And also with you,' responded the people. 'Thanks be to God,' and they went in peace. A tree was left in the soil as a sign of yesterday, today and tomorrow and the children were finally fed.

Memories keep moving, Patricia Woodbury told me, like her childhood river. The post boat still makes its daily run to deliver words onto land without road access. Spencer now has its own road to courier the mail in and out, but when Patricia used to come home for school holidays she travelled by river. If the train was late from Sydney and she missed the boat at Brooklyn she had to walk two kilometers from the ferry wharf to the convent where the Sisters of Mercy had an orphanage before trekking back to catch the boat the next day. I retraced her steps up Brooklyn Road past a pelican scratching its head and found the convent turned into a suite of apartments. I could see somebody's bed through the stained glass windows of the redbrick chapel, but the cross still sat atop the roof of the old 'nunnery' as the local who gave me directions described it. The selling of convents has been hard for Sister Patricia's community, too, but 'you can't hang on,' she said. 'You can't dig down deep and not come up.'

The convent in Goulburn where Theresa Woodbury died was still a school. A bare vine wrapped its arms around the high cross on the wall and a mother held her child in the pale pink iron lacework of the convent gate. Around the corner in the Paragon café was a black and white photograph of an eight-hour-day parade down Auburn Street the year Theresa turned thirteen. I looked at the girls wearing white dresses and the boys in their blazers watching the horse-drawn floats and wondered if the convent let the students join the crowd that day.

When Jean-Claude Colin imagined himself back in the home of Nazareth, he was already past middle age. At sixty-four he resigned as superior general of the Society of Mary. For the remaining two decades of his life he retreated in silence, tried eucharistic devotion, resisted change, wrote down what he saw, and eventually relinquished his most cherished hopes for the work he had founded. He disappeared into the Society and thus, in the words of Marist historian Jean Coste, 'Colin saved the Society of Mary.' What in the very heart of Nazareth's name possessed Colin in his twilight years to travel such a path?

John Jago wrote to his fellow Marists as superior general in Rome in 1986, 'We are to be extensions of Mary in her work of renewing the Church into a kingdom of mercy.' Forty years after Daniel Hurley's lament for children with no bread and twenty years on from Vatican II, Jago mentioned the lack of clerical vision for the laity. Sharing ministry in a hierarchical church wasn't a vision, he said. 'As Marists we must dedicate ourselves to the more important and radical task of transforming the Church into a communion and a people.' Jago asked not for more bread, or more hands to break it, but a different form of nourishment, 'one based not so much on hierarchy as on the ability to create an atmosphere in which people can recognise their gifts and have the courage to offer them for the task of the Kingdom.' In 2007 another superior general, Jan Hulshof, drew attention to Marist initiatives in Fiji: an ashram in Nadi and a retreat house called Nazareth outside Suva. Like inner-city desert places where people could come away for a while, like Marist Chapel in its founding days, Marist communities of contemplative prayer were fulfilling the vision for a child in search not of bread, but a mother's heart.

Maybe Colin needed somewhere to go when he felt lost and abandoned and confused, when he needed a wide lap and blanket and morning mists like soft kisses and blue-feathered wrens to wash his tears away. He came to Nazareth not to be fed, but to be healed from the abuse of his soul. When greed stole his body, and vanity divided his heart, and authoritarian systems held captive his mind, he came to Nazareth to learn to say *No*. He came to be bathed and wrapped and suckled with goodness and truth. He came to one who gave birth to a beautiful soul. He came to sit still and twirl and wake in her presence. He came to remember her body and face before going out to forget her again. He came home to treasure the gift of his life. He came for companionship that didn't mean bread. He came to find courage to trust the kookaburra's eyes and say *Yes* once more.

And after he turned and left Nazareth behind he flowed into another giving life to the land. He disappeared into deeper waters becoming, as it were, unknown. He gave everything he had to one who saw what he could become when he lost his way. He went up from Nazareth and found his new name.

Maybe the end of this story, which began in stone as a sacrament of remembering, is a sacrament of forgetting. Like Mary at the beginning of the church, the first cell of the church as Colin called Nazareth, the river is a sign of the creative act of disappearing.

> A teenage girl disappeared.
> Then her brother in a war.
> A mother faded and slipped away, too.
> Saint Thomas disappeared into a council.
> Religious fathers, mothers, sisters and brothers disappeared into the church.
> Wooden boxes disappeared, like liquid wax, into mystics and archetypes.
> Mothers and newborns grew into grandmothers and unaccompanied children.
> Seminaries disappeared and turned into universities.
> Language disappeared into the void.
> The void beat, *Listen*, and turned into a heart.
> A river turned and became unknown, then disappeared into an ocean.
> The moon heard, *Yes*, and washed up on dry land.

And so on, the stories of seventy years of adult faith in a church ever disappearing, eddy and flow ever becoming a place where the heart, like a mother's, just keeps expanding.

Timeline of an Academy

March 1945	Aquinas Academy founded by Austin M Woodbury SM
August 1945	End of Second World War
1970	Silver Jubilee of Aquinas Academy
1974	John Thornill SM appointed principal
1978	Commencement of baccalaureate in philosophy affiliated with University of Saint Thomas ('Angelicum'), Rome
February 1979	Death of Austin Woodbury
1981	Allan Connors SM appointed principal
1982	First Aquinas Academy summer school
1986	Baccalaureate programme suspended
1987	One-year term of Neville Byrne SM as principal
1988	Allan Connors SM reappointed principal
1991	Formal termination with Angelicum

1994	Kevin Bates SM appointed principal
1995	Fiftieth anniversary of Aquinas Academy
2000	Michael Whelan SM appointed principal
2005	Diamond Jubilee of Aquinas Academy
2007	Purchase of property 'Nazareth' on Colo River
2015	Seventieth anniversary of Aquinas Academy

Acknowledgements

I thank everyone who shared their time, homes, families, memories, photographs, music and paintings and trusted me to write their stories into this book: Anne Bailey, Pat Baker, Pat Barwell, Kevin Bates sm, John Begg sm, Marie Biddle rsj, Aileen Boon, Marita Brahe, Peter Carr, Catherine Cavanagh (née Jordan), Ross Coady, Allan Connors sm, Margaret Craw, Mary Crowe rsm, Graham English, Frank Featherstone, Tony Fitzgerald, Rosemary and Philippa Flannery, Gerard Hall sm, Catherine and Sam Hammond, Veronica Hilton, Luke Holohan sm, John Hosie, Johno Johnson, Pius Jones sm, Mary and Patrick Kirkwood, Joan McLean (née Smith), Lou Molloy sm, Celestine Pooley rsm, Aloysius Rego ocd, Tom Ryan sm, Elizabeth Sancataldo (née Mulcahy), Jack Soulsby sm, John Thornhill sm, Robert Tilley, Leonie Waterson, Michael Whelan sm, Erin White, Con Woodbury and Patricia Woodbury op. There are gaps, some omissions and my interpretations of the personal stories, but each has enriched and deepened the creative process of researching and writing this book.

For access to the archives of the Marist Fathers, I am indebted to Peter McMurrich sm, who along with Andrew Biddle gave me a happy home in Hunters Hill over the January I spent absorbed in the files of the Aquinas Academy and personal correspondence of Austin Woodbury. Peter answered every question I had about the Society of Mary at home and in Rome, looked up names of provincials, superior generals and assistant generals, identified cardinals and bishops from grainy photographs and scrawled signatures and sent me chapters from his masters thesis from the University of Sydney, *Not Angels, Nor Men Confirmed in Grace: The Marists in Post-Federation Australia*,

1892-1938, on the juniorates at Montbel and Mittagong. I have drawn frequently in this book from his publications, *Heritage and Memories: Portraits of Australian Marists, 1845-2001* and *The Harmonising Influence of Religion: St Patrick's Church Hill, 1840 to the Present.*

Keziah Doughty from Campion College library gave me access to the Austin Woodbury collection, which I used in Chapter Two for the text of Woodbury's 1929 speech in Wellington, New Zealand, on Action Française. In Chapter Four on the former St Joseph's Boys Home in Kincumber I am grateful for assistance and information from the museum volunteers at the St Joseph's Spirituality and Education Centre. In Chapter Seven Marita Brahe gave me copies of John Ogburn's writings. I also relied on essays by Emma Collerton in the catalogue from the exhibition she curated, *The Three O's: Orban, Olsen and Ogburn*, published by Orange Regional Gallery. In Chapter Eleven I consulted the State Library of New South Wales manuscript collections in the Mitchell Library for the personal papers of Terence Purcell. In Chapter Twelve I used the State Library of New South Wales sound recording of Caroline Jones's 1990 interview with Noel Rowe from the national radio programme, *The Search for Meaning.*

I drew extensively on the microfilm newspaper collection of the State Library of New South Wales and the National Library of Australia's Trove digital newspaper collection for articles in the *Australian Financial Review*, *Catholic Freeman's Journal*, *Catholic Weekly*, *Daily Mirror*, *Sydney Morning Herald* and the *Windsor and Richmond Gazette*. These collections complemented and expanded the archived articles from diocesan and metropolitan newspapers in the Aquinas Academy files.

Patricia Thompson rsj and Joanne Ng, respective archivists for the Sisters of St Joseph and Sisters of Mercy North Sydney, supplied details of Woodbury's sisters as well as a short history of St Patrick's business college. Chris Madden from the Holy Name Wahroonga Parish History group provided information on the Dominicans who taught at the Aquinas Academy and the Christian Growth Programme held in the parish.

I have quoted or mentioned several secondary sources in the book including Giuseppe Alberigo's *A Brief History of Vatican II*, GK Chesterton's *Saint Thomas Aquinas*, Jean-Louis Chrétien's *The Ark of Speech*, Bernard McGinn's *Thomas Aquinas's Summa Theologiae*,

Sandra M Schneider's *Religious Life in a New Millennium, Vol. I, Finding the Treasure: Locating Catholic Religious Life in a New Ecclesial and Cultural Context* and John Thornhill's *Sign and Promise: A Theology of the Church for a Changing World*.

On Action Française, Billot, Garrigou-Lagrange and the Maritains in Chapter Two, I used Michael Kerlin's chapter, 'Anti-Modernism and the elective affinity between politics and philosophy,' in Darrell Jodock's edited volume, *Catholicism Contending with Modernity: Roman Catholic Modernism and Anti-Modernism in Historical Context*, Brenna Moore's *Sacred Dread: Raïssa Maritain, the Allure of Suffering, and the French Catholic Revival (1905-1944)* and Richard Peddicord's *The Sacred Monster of Thomism: An Introduction to the Life and Legacy of Réginald Garrigou-Lagrange*.

In Chapter Four on John Anderson, Paddy Ryan, Roger Pryke and BA Santamaria, Chapter Eight on the Gorman affair and Chapter Thirteen on Pryke's formation course for nuns, I have drawn on Edmund Campion's *Rockchoppers: Growing Up Catholic in Australia*, Bruce Duncan's *Crusade or Conspiracy: Catholics and the Anti-Communist Struggle in Australia*, James Franklin's *Corrupting the Youth: A History of Philosophy in Australia* and Francis Ravel Harvey's *Traveller to Freedom: The Roger Pryke Story*.

Bernard McGinn's *The Flowering of Mysticism: Men and Women in the New Mysticism 1200-1350* was my source on Mechthild of Magdeburg, Hadewijch of Antwerp and the beguines in Chapter Nine. References to Constance FitzGerald's articles, 'Impasse and Dark Night,' in Tilden Edwards' edited collection, *Living with Apocalypse: Spiritual Resources for Social Compassion* and 'From Impasse to Prophetic Hope: Crisis of Memory,' *CTSA Proceedings* 64 (2009), appear in Chapters Ten, Thirteen and Fourteen. I have quoted from *Etty: The Letters and Diaries of Etty Hillesum 1941-1943*, edited by Klaas AD Smelik and translated by Arnold J Pomerans in Chapter Thirteen, and in Chapter Fifteen from Jean Coste's *A Contemporary Reading of Foundational Marist Images*, which John Thornhill gave me both for my research and personal enrichment. Quotes from Thomas Merton in Chapter Fourteen come from the epilogue, 'Fire Watch, July 4, 1952,' in *The Sign of Jonas* and a passage in *Disputed Questions* from Michael Whelan's seminar handout. The story of

Chapter Fifteen was inspired by Maisie Cavanagh's 'Deerubbin and Colo' from her collection, *The Rock and the Tree*.

The texts of papal encyclicals, unless quoted from a newspaper, come from Papal Encyclicals Online, http://www.papalencyclicals.net. The text of *Perfectae Caritatis* can be found in the Vatican archive of council documents, http://www.vatican.va/archive/hist_councils/ii_vatican_council/documents/vat-ii_decree_19651028_perfectae-caritatis_en.html.

Naomi Shihab Nye's poem, 'Kindness,' which I quoted in part in Chapter One, is from her collection, *Words under the Words: Selected Poems*. I am grateful to Gerri Power who first shared 'Kindness' with me in her Anam Cara writing journey, and to Grace Bower who knitted kindness into my sabbatical. Jay Winter's work on liturgical silence can be found in his edited volume, *Shadows of War: A Social History of Silence in the Twentieth Century*.

For opportunity, encouragement and companionship, I thank Vesna Drapac who taught me to be a historian and whose first book, *War and Religion: Catholics in the Churches of Occupied Paris*, taught me to see Catholics, Michael Whelan and Marie Biddle who made the Aquinas Academy my new spiritual home, John Fairbrother and Vaughan Park Anglican Retreat Centre who knew there would one day be a book, Sally Longley who has helped me to listen and Di Mackenzie who I first met at the Academy in a circle of forgiveness and who introduced me to a circle of prayer companions.

Finally, I wish to thank Brendan Moran and Anthony Reeder who clarified and corrected early versions of the manuscript. This book began in Patti Miller's 'True Stories' course at Faber Writing Academy and I thank Patti as well as the writers in her class who encouraged the words on the page as they took shape.

INDEX

A

A Brief History of Vatican II. See Giuseppe Alberigo
Abbot Hawkins, 139.
Action Française, 11, 12, 13, 18, 158, 159.
Aeterni Patris, 6.
AIDS, 122.
Alberigo, Giuseppe, 74, 158.
Anderson, John 30, 159.
Angelicum, the 7, 12, 43, 73, 75, 78, 84, 85, 155.
apostolic delegate. See Marella, Paolo.
Aquinas Academy, passim.
Archbishop Little, 110, 120.
Aristotle, 21, 75, 76, 77, 93, 94.
Australian Catholic University, 123, 135.
Australian Financial Review, 82, 158.

B

baccalaureate, 86, 88, 90, 92, 113, 115, 119, 155.
Baker, Pat, 101.
Bates, Kevin, 2, 8, 120, 122, 128, 136, 156, 157.
Batten, Reginald, 73, 74, 82, 137.
Baulkham Hills, 36, 134, 135, 136, 138.
Begg, John 52, 157.
Belloc, Hilaire, 2.
Bernanos, George, 135.
bible study, 144.
Billot, Louis, 12.
Bishop Muldoon. See Muldoon, Thomas.
Blacktown, 132, 149.
Boland, Don, 46, 113, 115.
Boon, Aileen, 47, 157.
Boston, 126, 129, 130.
Biddle, Marie, 3, 133, 144, 157, 160.
Brahe, Marita 63, 70, 157, 158.
British Israel World Foundation, 82.
Browne, Michael, 73, 74, 82, 137.
Buber, 143, 144.
Buckley, Joseph 78, 87.
Burmese refugee, 114.
Butler, Gregory, 44, 47, 73.

C

Callinan, Karl, 119.
Campion College, 66, 158.
Campion Hall, 65.

Capuchin, 81.
Cardinal Cushing, 130.
Cardinal Garrone, 84.
Carmelite, 87, 96, 115, 116, 117, 118.
Catalyst for Renewal, 145.
catechetics, 119, 123, 129, 131, 132.
Catholic Universe, 9
Catholic University Students' Guild, 11
Catholic Weekly, 21, 24, 29, 30, 31, 32, 34, 46, 51, 59, 60, 80, 82, 91, 99, 96, 97, 100, 101, 109, 112, 121, 127, 131, 140, 149, 158.
Cavanagh, Maisie, 146
Centre for Pastoral and Social Ministry at the University of Notre Dame, 110.
Cézanne, 66, 68.
charismatic prayer group, 139, 140.
Charismatic renewal, 130.
Christian Growth Programme, 96, 98, 103, 105, 109, 113, 116, 121, 123, 126, 132, 158.
Chesterton, GK, 2, 5, 7, 158.
Church Hill, 10, 115, 119, 126, 158.
Clancy, Archbishop, 110, 112.
Cleophas, 98.
Colin, Jean-Claude, 124, 128, 150, 152.
Collins, Pat, 123.
Colo River, 138, 150, 151, 156.
Communists, 31, 60.
Congar, Yves, viii, 88.
Congregation of the Doctrine of the Faith, 112.
Connors, Allan, 96, 98, 97, 101, 102, 103, 105, 107, 111, 121, 124, 126, 155, 157.
contemplative, 67, 113, 114, 115, 139, 140, 145, 146, 147, 153.
Contemplative Rhythm, 144.
Coste, Jean 153, 159.

Council of Trent, 87.
Cowhan, Lucy, 87
CUSA House, 31, 32.
Cyr, Alcime, 77.

D

Dante, 13.
Daughters of Our Lady of the Sacred Heart, 17.
Daughters of St Paul, 129.
Davis, Charles, 139.
de Lubac, Henri, 77.
de Waal, Esther, 144.
Deegan, Geoff, 81, 113, 115.
Developing Your Own Spirituality, 138, 139.
Diary of a Country Priest, 135.
Die Reichspost, 19.
Divini Illius Magistri, 32.
Dollfuss, Engelbert 19, 20.
Doc, the. See Woodbury, Austin
Domain. See Speakers corner.
Dominian, Edith, 101.
Dominian, Jack, 99, 100, 101, 102, 109, 110, 111, 112.
Dominican, 6, 12, 23, 25, 27, 43, 44, 46, 56, 61, 66, 73, 78, 81, 85, 87, 95, 104, 114, 117, 118, 120, 137, 140, 158.
Donovans, 1.
Douglas Social Credit, 82.
Doyles, 1.
Duquesne University, 136, 141.

E

earthquake, 14, 25.
Eliot, TS 147.
encyclical, 2, 6, 7, 19, 21, 31, 60, 73,

77, 100, 142, 160.
English, Colleen, 47.
English, Graham, 67, 157.
enrollments, 29, 81, 112, 113, 149, 150.

F

Fascist, 7, 19, 20, 31, 60.
Fernández, Aniceto, 81.
Finding Faith in Troubled Times, 123.
First World War, 4, 7.
FitzGerald, Constance, 96, 138, 145, 146.
Fitzgerald, Lawrence, 43, 73.
Fitzgerald, Terry, 85, 86, 100, 102, 113, 119.
Fitzgerald, Tony,101, 157.
Flanders, 4.
Flannery, Rosemary, 88, 157.
Fordham University, 130.
Formative Spirituality, 109, 136, 137.
Fra Angelico, 65.
Freethought Society. See Anderson, John.
Friedman, Maurice, 140
Fruitful and Responsible Love, 111.

G

Gill, Alan, 100, 111.
Garrigou-Lagrange, Reginald, 12, 13, 14, 18, 43, 78, 159.
Geelong, 121.
Gestetner, 24, 42, 99.
Ghiberti, 13.
Gillen, John, 102.

Gilroy, Archbishop later Cardinal, 19, 21, 22, 32, 33, 34, 44, 45, 46, 66, 72, 1.
Glenorie, 4.
Gloucester Street, 23, 59, 71, 79, 80, 92, 123, 140.
Glynn, John, 80, 81.
Gorman affair, 99, 114, 159.
Gorman, Margaret, 80.
Goulburn, 2, 5, 101, 152.
gracious choice, 143.
Greenberg, Clement, 67.
Greenmeadows, 6, 10, 14, 18, 125.
Gregorian, the, 12, 31.
Griffiths, Bede 123.

H

Hadewijch of Antwerp, 90, 159.
Hall, Gerard, 109, 122, 132, 157.
Hammond, Catherine, 129, 135, 147.
Harcombe, James, 72, 81.
Harvest Magazine, 147.
Hawkesbury, 1.
head and teeth spirituality, 140.
Healy, Gabrielle, 105.
Hearn, Barbara, 65, 66, 109, 104.
Heidegger, Martin, 143, 144, 147.
Henry George League, 82.
hidden and, as it were, unknown, 125.
Hillesum, Etty, 137, 146, 159.
Hindu-Christian-Buddhist relations, 122.
Hitchen, William, 5.
Holley, John, 6.
Holohan, Luke, 129
Hunter, Hughena, 10
Hulshof, Jan, 153.
Humanae vitae, 101, 142.

Humani Generis, 77.
Hunters Hill, 5, 9, 19, 70, 82, 88, 89, 96, 98, 99, 108, 110, 117, 118, 120, 122, 130, 143, 153.
Hurley, Daniel 10, 18, 19, 20, 22, 30, 71, 72, 73, 153.

I

Ignatian spirituality, 126.
Institut Catholique, 45.
Institute of Faith Education in Brisbane, 133.
International House of Studies, 78.
International Theological Commission, 78.

J

Jago, John 99, 100, 110, 140, 153.
John Paul II, 61, 77, 89.
John XXIII, 74, 84.
Johnson, Grove, 34.
Johnson, Johno, 51, 64, 120, 157.
Jones, Caroline, 122, 158.
Josephites, 91, 134.
Jung, CG, 109, 112, 126.
juniorate, 5, 6, 22, 158.

K

Kincumber, 36, 37, 114, 138, 158.
King, Tony, 6, 14.
Kirkwood, Mary and Patrick, 104, 157.
Korean Uniting Church Choir, 123.
Küng, Hans, 89.

L

La Paroisse, 124.
League of Nations, 7.
lectio divina, 141, 144.
Lewis, CS, 65.
Little Company of Mary, 25, 135.
Lochinvar Sisters of St Joseph, 104.
London University, 29.
Lonergan, Bernard, 106.
Lopez, Rosa, 102.
Lacan, Jacques, 137.
Lussier, Irénée, 46.
Lyndhurst Academy, 33, 34.

M

Maloneys, 1.
Mangrove, 1, 37.
Marist, *passim*.
Marist Chapel, 119, 149
Maritain, Jacques, 12, 13, 14, 21, 33, 106, 159.
Maritain, Raïssa
Marella, Paolo, 34.
Marx/Marxism, 93, 94, 140.
Matisse, 62, 63, 64, 65, 72, 76
Maurras, Charles, 11.
McCaffrey, Eugene, 116.
McAuley, James 86, 113, 135.
McGinn, Bernard, 87, 90, 158, 159.
Mechthild of Magdeburg, 90, 159.
meditatio/meditation, 47, 122, 140, 141.
Menin Gate, 11.
Mercy, Sister of, 2, 5, 24, 36, 37, 41, 90, 92, 93, 94, 99, 101, 152, 158.
mercy, 90, 105, 125, 128, 151, 153.
Merton, Thomas, 114, 115, 118, 146, 150, 159.
Mittagong, 5, 6, 7, 10, 17, 37, 158.
Mixed Blessings, 123.

Molloy, Lou, 48, 153
Monaghan, James 5.
Montbel, 5, 7, 74, 158.
Mooney, John Ignatius 5.
Mount St Mary's, 6.
Mount Street, 135.
Muldoon, Thomas, Bishop, 34, 35, 37, 38, 73, 79, 80, 112, 120.
Murphy-O'Connor, Cormac 145.
mystical, 12, 90, 95, 96, 140, 146.
mystical and ascetical theology, 140.
Mystical Body of Christ, 141.
mystical heart, 139ff, 145, 150, 151.

N

National Catholic Education Commission, 133.
Nazareth, 146, 147, 148, 149, 150, 152
Nazi, 19, 20, 66, 137.
Nelson, Alice, 113, 115.
Neothomism, 87.
New Norcia. See Sr Hildebrand
Newman Society, 33, 88.
Non abbiamo bisogno, 20.

O

O'Connor, Flannery, 138.
O'Dwyer, John, 81.
O'Malley, John 74.
Ogburn, John 63, 64, 67, 68, 69, 158.
Orama, 9.
Orban, 64, 65, 66, 67, 158.

P

Panikkar, Raimon, 122.
Passionist, 114, 117.
Patricia. See Woodbury, Patricia.
Paulian Association, 105.
Paulist, 81.
Perfectae Caritatis, 135, 160.
philosophy, *passim*.
Picasso, 68.
Pius XI, 6, 7, 9, 10, 11, 19, 21, 31, 34.
Pius XII, 34, 77, 146.
Pooley, Celestine, 86, 91, 93, 108, 116, 124, 127, 153.
Pontifical Faculties, 101.
Pope Leo XIII, 6.
Pope Paul VI, 74, 100, 105, 135.
Pope Pius XII, 6, 34, 77, 146.
Presentation Order in Lismore, 57.
Proposals for a New Sexual Ethic, 100.

Q

Quadragesimo anno, 60.

R

Rahner, Karl, 88.
Rausch, John, 5, 6, 7, 10, 12, 18.
Rego, Aloysius 114, 130, 157.
Religion and Personality, 141.
Rembrandt, 69.
Rerum novarum, 60.
Reynolds, Garry, 113.
Russell, Anthony, 45.
Ryan, PJ, Paddy, 31, 32, 33, 46, 159.
Ryan, Barbara, 127.
Ryan, Tom, 52, 109, 119, 120, 125, 133, 136, 147, 157.

S

Saint John of the Cross, 96, 116, 118, 146.
Saint Teresa of Ávila, 115, 118, 140.
Saint Thérèse of Lisieux, 45, 118.
Saint Thomas, passim.
Salvation Army Sydney Congress Hall Songster Brigade, 123.
San Francisco Theological Seminary, 104.
Sancta Sophia College, 88, 135.
Sancataldo, Elizabeth, 35, 44, 47, 157.
Santamaria, BA 33, 159.
Schillebeeckx, Edward, 88, 117, 118.
Schneiders, Sandra, 95, 96, 139.
Schuschnigg, Kurt, 20.
Second World War, 53, 75, 155.
Sheed, Frank, 34.
seminary, vii, 5, 6, 12, 14, 15, 17, 20, 21, 22, 31, 43, 44, 60, 66, 73, 7, 92, 104, 106, 114, 121, 125, 132, 133, 135, 139, 140, 141, 142.
Shakeshafts, 1.
Sign and Promise, 89, 159.
Silverstream, 18, 125.
Sister of St Joseph, 3, 36, 47, 101, 104, 133, 134, 158.
Sister Philomena, 24, 42, 90, 98, 99, 01.
Smith, Colin, 105.
Smith, John Venard, 116.
Smith, Joan, 41, 43, 47, 157.
Social reconstruction, 31.
Society of Mary, 6, 22, 30, 71, 72, 78, 86, 104, 147, 153.
Soulsby, Jack, 52, 58, 60, 63, 64, 114, 120, 140, 153, 157.
Speaker's Corner, 32, 61.
Sr Aiden, 57.
Sr Hildebrand Russell, 75.
Sr Koska, 57.
Sr Mary de Sales Daly, 57.
Sr Mary Kieran, 57.
St Gregory Chorale, 104, 105.
St Mary's Cathedral Choir, 38, 123.
St Patrick's, 10, 11, 18, 20, 22, 23, 24, 30, 31, 38, 42, 73, 86, 88, 90, 91, 98, 100, 102, 103, 111, 119, 120, 121, 123, 126, 144, 158.
St Patrick's Chorale, 123.
St Vincent de Paul Society, 127.
Sussex Street, 56, 58.
Sydney Armenian Church Choir, 123.
Sydney Jewish Choral Society, 123.
Sydney Morning Herald, 5, 64, 80, 99, 100, 111, 158.

T

Te Wairua Tapu (Holy Spirit) Maori Choir, 123.
The Academician, 48, 49.
The Framework of a Christian State, 58.
The Rocks, 59, 67, 103, 119.
The Seven Storey Mountain, 115.
Thornhill, John, 84, 86, 89, 91, 92, 96, 100, 120, 125, 140, 157.
Toynbee, Arnold, 75.
Toongabbie, vii, 15, 17, 18, 19, 20, 22, 25, 43, 44, 60, 66, 77, 78, 81, 92, 121, 126.
Transcendentalism, 88.
Trinity College, Dublin, 132.

U

Umileniye, 143.
University and University Colleges Act, 30.

University of Notre Dame in Fremantle, the, 128.

V

Van Kaam, Adrian, 136, 137, 141, 142.
Varroville, 115, 116, 117.
Vatican Council, 14, 67, 74, 78, 85, 126.
Vatican II, 74, 78, 87, 88, 95, 96, 97, 98, 104, 109, 104,130, 135, 139, 145, 147, 150, 153, 158.

W

Wahroonga, 43, 66, 73, 104, 109, 158.
Walesa, Lech, 61.
Waterson, Leonie, 98, 102, 105, 157.
Webber, John, 43.
Weston School of Theology, 126.
Whelan, Dympna, 147, 150.
Whelan, Michael, vii, 3, 51, 109, 136, 138, 139, 144, 147, 156.
White, Erin, 67, 122, 157.
Whiteheads, the, 110, 121.
Winter, Jay, 3, 160.
Wittgenstein, Ludwig ,134
Wojtyla, Karol, 61.
Women's Auxiliary Australian Air Force. See Smith, Joan.
Woodbury, Austin, 1, 2, 4, 5, 6, 8, 9, 10, 11, 17, 23, 24, 25, 26, 27, 36, 37, 48, 58, 61, 62, 83, 86, 88, 145, 155, 157, 158.
Woodbury, Cecily, 17, 26, 83, 84.
Woodbury, Con, 157.
Woodbury, Patricia, 23, 25, 27, 42, 48, 99, 102, 110, 119, 120, 152, 157.
Woodbury, Stephen, 4, 5, 8, 11, 25, 37.
Woodburys, 1
Woodbury, Theresa, 2, 8.
Workers' School of Social Reconstruction, 31.

Y

Ypres, 11.

Z

Zen and the Birds of Appetite, 114.
Zen Buddhism, 142.

Lightning Source UK Ltd.
Milton Keynes UK
UKHW041355241019
352163UK00007B/32/P